# The Soul of the Leader

## Success with Authenticity, Integrity and Empathy

Arthur P. Ciaramicoli, Ed.D., Ph.D.
with Jim Crystal, Founder of The Revelry Group

Open Books

Published by Open Books

Copyright © 2019 by Arthur P. Ciaramicoli

Interior design by Siva Ram Maganti

ISBN-13: 978-1948598125

In recent years' every colleague, friend and player and coach I know has expressed deep concern about the lack of ethical leadership in our society. Dr. Ciaramicoli's book is full of poignant stories of leadership failure and leadership success. He teaches us how to combine profit and character, how to lead others to their full potential and how to live a life of truth and success. If we all take in a bit of his wisdom our organizations and our lives will be better.

—Lawrence Brady,
Faculty in Sport Management, Cortland State college

As a director and leader of behavioral health programs I have worked with many students and employees who have been disheartened by toxic leaders. In my private practice I have encountered numerous leaders in the business world who seem utterly confused as to how to lead effectively. Dr. Ciaramicoli's book teaches us how to incorporate AIE leadership into all aspects of our lives, not only as leaders in business but also as leaders in our own homes. My hope is that his book will become the bible of soulful leadership. This book is a gem!

—Robert Cherney, Ph.D.,
Chief Psychologist,
Advocates Community Counseling Services,
Framingham, Massachusetts

As a leader in what has traditionally been a man's world I understand the difficulties in how to convince those at the top that AIE leadership will increase profits and happiness. Dr. Ciaramicoli's book is not only filled with wisdom and the path to balanced success but is a manual that proves, through his consulting and through his citing of credible research, that authenticity, integrity and empathy are the only was to achieve and profit with health and joy.

—Mary Bethony, M.D.,
CEO of All About Women

I have been in leadership positions in the technology industry for over 30 years. I have worked for and with toxic leaders and soulful leaders. I have always wondered throughout my career how it comes about that some leaders create harmful cultures while others create happy, creative cultures. Dr. Ciaramicoli provides the answers that all leaders need to understand in order to lead with joy, creativity and resilience. I am sending a copy to all my trusted colleagues.

—Richard Werner,
President & Chief Operating Officer,
RC Werner & Associates, LLC,
Consultant to the data center industry

Dr. Ciaramiccoli's latest work captures the essence of true leadership shining a brighter light on our cultural evolution; the shift away from a power model towards valuing Divine feminine principles. His passion for redirecting our cultural view of business towards valuing interiority, empathy, vulnerability and soul above wealth and status helps us take critical strides towards redefining our intrinsic idea of what it means to be responsible leaders. Dr. Ciarmicoli makes you not only want to be a better leader but shows you how!

—Maryanne Comaroto, Ph.D.,
Relationship Expert,
Author and Founder of The National Action Organization;
Changing the way our culture values women

*The Soulful Leader* provides the blueprint for high-level leadership. This book reveals remedies for our troubled times. Using the elements of authenticity, integrity and empathy, the Soulful Leader develops a team fully committed to his or her vision. This creates both extraordinary performance and high-level human living.

—Tom Marcoux,
Spoken Word Strategist and Executive Coach,

Speaker-Author of 50+ Books,
CEO, leading teams in U.K., India and USA,
GetTheBigYES.com

*The Soulful Leader* is, in my opinion, another celebrating milestone in Dr. Ciaramicoli's contribution towards making our world a better place. Dr. Ciaramicoli's wisdom and experience captures and accents ethical behaviour and raises awareness and prompts an increase in moral judgments that is so severely absent in our current society. Dr. Ciaramicoli emphasises the need for empathy within the human spirit and within each individual, especially leaders, all across the world and across varying professions. As an organisational psychotherapist in private practice for the last 13 years, and having worked for large corporations throughout my 22 year career in the mental health industry, I strongly recommend Dr. Ciaramicoli's book - not just to leaders of corporations and politicians (especially), but also to everyone who has the ultimate goal of attaining a soulful and meaningful life - both private and professional - through empathy, emotional growth and self-actualisation, whilst still contributing positively to society and to their loved ones' lives.

—Dr. Jane Leigh, PhD.
Clinical Mental Health Consultant,
Author of *My Nine Lives - A Psychotherapist's Journey from Victim to Survivor* and Director of
DJL Counselling Consultancy, Melbourne, Australia

"Only passions, great passions, can elevate the soul to Great Things."

—French Philosopher,
Denis Diderot

To Ariana and Carmela, your open hearts enliven my
soul every day

# Contents

# Foreword

I HAVE BEEN A coach and mentor to young men and women since 1983. I learned early, from my years at Assumption College, that the most respected of all my peers were the people who demonstrated exceptional character on and off the field.

Nothing has changed my mind over the last 35 years. Dr. Ciaramicoli has captured all that I believe creates successful and ethical leadership in all spheres of life.

Whether as a parent, coach, teacher, CEO or CFO the formula of Authenticity, Integrity and Empathy (AIE) leadership captures the necessary ingredients to develop the potential of all those we hope will become tomorrow's leaders.

As I read *The Soulful Leader* I thought to myself that our nation and world would soar to success if everyone in leadership could value AIE.

Dr. Ciaramicoli's insight and wisdom give the reader poignant examples of how to live a personal and professional life of balance, and how to pass on the AIE formula to those we are fortunate to lead. Read this book, study this book and practice the AIE formula for a better life and for creating a better world.

—Brian Kelly, Dick Corbett
Head Football Coach at the University of Notre Dame

# Introduction

SHORTLY AFTER ARETHA FRANKLIN's passing I was meeting with one of my clients who is a world-class musician and a college professor of music. He was trying to define what it is about Aretha, Jennifer Hudson, Lady Gaga and others that make them so special.

*"They are so passionate, they inspire, they lead us as musicians to play better, to play with more emotion; they are just so incredibly soulful."*

He went on to say that soul is not definable but rather something that is emotionally experienced. He said the great ones lead by example.

*"You can't play with them without wanting to be your best in their presence; even when you're not on stage you feel more soulful."*

AIE (authenticity, integrity and empathy) leaders, whether in music, in business, in politics or within their families, touch the soul in a lasting way.

## An Early Lesson

When I was eight years old my parents, my brother and I were preparing to attend a family wedding. I heard my parents talking about the people who would likely attend. My father commented with a touch of sarcasm, "I suppose the great lawyer will be there." I immediately chimed in and asked, "Why would you talk that way about him? He gets to go to court and put the bad guys in jail." My mother, in her infinite wisdom, then asked me if I thought the lawyer would remember my name, or anyone else in our family, when we went to the wedding. I said yes, and she predicted that the local butcher would remember my name and everyone else in our family as well. He was a generous man who frequently gave food to the poor. He had met me only a few times. She also predicted that the lawyer would not call us by name, even though he had attended many gatherings at which our family was present. Of course she was right. That night I asked her how she was able to predict his insincerity. "He has no heart. He's unfriendly and arrogant. On the other hand, you cannot be in the butcher's company without being happy. He loves everybody, and everybody loves him, and people are happy working for him."

We know on a visceral, emotional level when someone has soul. Whether it be the local market owner or a musician playing with a soulful singer, we feel elated and energized when we encounter it. Allow me to try to define this abstract quality with a bit more clarity.

## What Makes Up the Soul

Soul is the invisible, intangible part of every human being that yearns for attachment to something deeper and broader than what we perceive to be ourselves. **A person who is soulful lives with purpose and expresses a desire to be of service. He or she is not primarily motivated by status or image but has a natural interest in making the most of all they encounter.** Soulful people lead with passion, and they are intimately aware of the structure of their organization. They are interested in motivating from the bottom up, not from the top down. They know who cleans their office, who mows the lawn, who fixes their computers, who serves the food; they know the secretaries and the receptionists. They speak to everyone, and no person is seen as less valuable than anyone else. Soulful people lead balanced lives, work with intensity, play with abandonment, but they also know how to turn down the dial and simply enjoy life. They have an inherent love of young people; they love to educate, to witness the blossoming of young talent. They are the voice of reason in the face of conflict; they are not quick to react, rather thoughtful contributors. They know how to listen, as they are genuinely interested in understanding not only those who are like them, but also those who on the surface seem different; they are known for finding common ground.

They take in information from diverse sources. They expect to continue to gain information about themselves, their world and the human condition throughout their lives. They expect to revise theories and change perspectives as new learning takes place. They are not wedded to one way of thinking, one way of being or one way of leading. They realize and willingly accept that in order to live a healthy, high-achieving life they must adapt to change, as they will be constantly faced with new situations that require adjustments. They understand that those to whom they are closest will also grow and change, and they welcome their evolution. They live their lives with an open heart and an open mind.

## Authenticity, Wealth and Performance

Many in the corporate world have come to believe that they have to sacrifice ethics and integrity for wealth and status. A study examining the long-term stock performance of companies that had won the Corporate Health Achievement Award, an annual prize that the American College of Occupational and Environmental

Medicine has awarded since 1996 to recognize organizations with exemplary health, safety, and environmental programs, revealed that the those organizations substantially outperformed the returns of the S&P 500 from 2001 to 2014—often by 200 percentage points or more. Companies with value-driven cultures also showed quantifiable benefits.[1] Evidence gathered by professor John Quelch of the Harvard Business School suggests that they also may have lower healthcare costs, less absenteeism, better employee retention, fewer workplace injuries, stronger growth, improved corporate reputations, and, of course, better stock performance.[2]

Lady Geek, a consultant company based in London, rates companies across the globe for the degree of empathy present in their corporate culture. They find a clear correlation between empathy and financial success.

Interestingly, US banks are capitalizing on the benefits of empathy with their clients, scoring 50% higher than banks in the UK.

Research by the London group indicates that businesses are more productive and more profitable when leaders act ethically and interact with staff and clients in considerate ways. The top 10 companies in the most recent Lady Geek Global Empathy Index (2015) increased their value more than twice as much as those companies rated in the bottom 10. They also generated 50% more earnings. The top 10 companies increased 6% this year, while the bottom 10 companies dropped 9%.

Research has proven that when we live within the AIE value system we create an inner calm that is sensed by others, allowing us to actualize our potential by freeing energy from the stress of compromising oneself or

1. American College of Occupational and Environmental Medicine. Corporate Health Achievement Award. 2014

2. Parmar, Belinda. Harvard Review. 11/27/15

one's values. Leaders who demonstrate AIE leadership are attractive to others; they relax those who work for them and their customers/clients as the need to be on guard lessens, freeing people to make mistakes and participate without the worry of being graded punitively.

**AIE leaders cause positive brain changes in themselves and in others, creating a spirited atmosphere that naturally allows productivity and financial and market results to rise accordingly.**

AIE relaxes customers and clients as it breeds trust and lessens the idea that leaders have ulterior motives and simply care about their personal gain. Rather than anticipating a sales process they experience an individual who is willing to listen to the needs and concerns of the clients they serve.

Harvard Business School Professor Bill George and his team conducted in-person interviews with 125 leaders while also reviewing 1,000 studies to determine how authentic leaders are developed. These studies, featured in his book *Discover Your True North*, determined that authentic leaders are open to new challenges and new learning. They lead meaningful lives, are true to themselves and to their values. They are genuine, moral, self-disciplined and display excellent character.

Most importantly, they are committed to self-growth.[3]

## The Inspired Actions of a Soulful Leader

A leader who thinks, acts and behaves in a soulful manner inspires others to do the same, essentially developing a **soulful culture. Our nervous systems talk to each other, and simple human interactions can**

---

3. George, Bill. *Discover Your True North*. Jossey-Bass, New York. 2015

**change brain chemistry. Empathic interactions of a collective can change the brain chemistry of an entire organization.**

A good leader has the attention of everyone. When people sense arrogance, dismissal, poor interpersonal skills, lack of compassion, and most importantly lack of integrity, the spirit of an organization suffers dramatically. Researchers from Princeton showed that leaders who are judged to be competent but lack warmth cause envy and resentment in employees. Amy Cuddy of Harvard Business School conducted research demonstrating that leaders who relate with warmth are more effective than people who relate with aggression. Kindness and warmth create trust; trust releases the bonding hormone oxytocin, which creates a desire to connect with others.

Oxford University researchers accessed and reviewed hundreds of published studies focusing on the relationship between happiness and kindness. 21 studies indicated that kindness makes us happier, and happy employees are more productive at work.[4]

Further research of 51,836 leaders by Jack Zenger and Joseph Folkman found that leaders who are disliked have a one in 2000 chance of being considered a good leader.[5]

AIE leaders gain favorability by not compromising their values, which exudes a purity of intention and a genuine concern for the mission statement of the businesses they administrate.

When I have consulted with corporations I have noticed that as leaders adopt the AIE perspective, not only through understanding but through actions,

---

4. Forbes. *How Purposeful Kindness Can Make You A Better Leader*. David Stuart and Todd Nordstrom. 10/24/2018

5. Zenger, Jack and Folkman, Joseph. *Bad Leaders Can Change Their Spots*. Harvard Business Review.1/24/2013

employees begin to mirror their approach and behavior. Why? Because people simply feel better when we relate in compassionate, mindful ways. We change our brains, which makes us happier and more creative. Creativity as a part of successful strategizing increases as behavior becomes more authentic. We become agents for change, encouraging the potential of an entire group or organization.

**Sidebar: Please take the AIE and Performance Addiction Questionnaires in the appendix and then again when you finish reading the book.**

# 1.

## You Get What You Give: Creating a Soulful Organization through Goodness and Serving Others

*"We are one of the first companies to be recognized as leaders of a global movement of companies using business as a force for good."*

—The Revelry Group

I MET WITH A new client the other day that had been referred for stress and anxiety. I entered my waiting room and greeted a tall, handsome, fit man in a designer suit. He stood and shook my hand with great emphasis.

*"I'm messed up, Doc. Can't get it straight."*

He told me that he was having an affair with a thirty-five-year-old woman; he was now 56. His wife was unaware and he was trying to decide whether to leave his wife or stay in the marriage. He had twin daughters, both in local Boston colleges. He told me that he has always been a self-absorbed person. "I do things my way, and my wife has always told me I am selfish. I'm a smart guy, very successful, but I want to be happy, and this affair is the only thing that excites me right now."

## Hedonistic Pursuits

**Sex can be binding and blinding,** especially in the early phases of a relationship. Rob has never learned how to connect in an empathic manner, as a result he has never experienced the benefits of deep connections. **Empathic connections change our brain chemistry and make us happy and secure**. When we give and receive empathy we produce the magical neurochemical oxytocin. Oxytocin reduces anxiety, inflammation, and addictive cravings, while increasing trust, generosity, calmness and a sense of well-being. It also protects against heart disease, and aids in recovery from illness.

Rob, like many individuals in the corporate world with money and power, has come to believe that he can pursue happiness through possessions, status, sex and extravagant vacations.

Research has revealed that happiness cannot be pursued directly. If it could be attained by acquisitions or achievement alone, then I would be out of business, as I work with many successful business individuals who find happiness to be elusive.

If you are a self-absorbed leader who seldom invests in listening to and caring for your employees, then you will rarely derive sustainable pleasure from your work.

When I was a young man, a few years after becoming a licensed clinical psychologist, my parents visited my office at a near-by hospital one Friday night after I'd finished with patients. My office was at the end of a long corridor. A man who was cleaning offices greeted my parents as they got off the elevator at the other end of the hallway, and my father stopped to speak with him before they approached my office. Of course, as a young man I couldn't wait for my folks to see the sign on my door: *Arthur P. Ciaramicoli, Chief Clinical Psychologist.*

My dad congratulated me and soon asked me if I knew the man at the end of the corridor. I said that I did not, and he instructed me to go down the hall and introduce myself. "Ask him his name, find out if he has a wife, children and remember what he tells you, he is your co-worker."

Mario, a Brazilian immigrant, and I became friends from that day onward. We would take time for coffee at the end of the day and he would share stories of how he'd brought his family to America, how grateful he was to be working at the hospital, and how much he appreciated all the opportunities he and his wife encountered as a result of being in the United States. In truth, I learned far more from him than he ever learned from me. My dad gave me a gift that Friday evening. His lesson: be humble, don't get carried away with status, and engage everyone in your environment. He knew, from owning his own business, that a giving nature would reap far more benefits for all involved than self-absorbed preoccupations.

## Giving Changes Our Brains

A classic study by Allan Luks, director of Big Brothers and Sisters of New York City, found that people who are giving on a regular basis are 10 times more likely to be healthy than people who do not. The so-called "helpers high" leads to a release of healthy brain chemicals, which in turn lead to altruistic behavior.

People who are generous in relationships are more likely to have excellent health than those who are self-absorbed. Giving behavior wires the brain for pleasure, causing a pleasing neurochemical change. Researchers from the National Institute of Health examined functional MRIs of people who gave to charities. They discovered that giving stimulates the mesolimbic pathway, the reward center in the brain that releases feel good endorphins that elicit happiness and joy.[1]

People who engage in random acts of kindness are happier, live longer; have lower blood pressure and less stress. In addition, happy people are more creative, more productive and, most importantly, they increase team cooperation and team spirit.

Harvard researchers have found that acts of altruism spread by three degrees—from one person, to another, to another. One person acting in a giving manner within a company can positively influence dozens of other workers.[2]

Interestingly, when people are given monetary rewards to be giving, they give less. Once we monetize the natural tendency to give, it changes perception; generosity is no longer coming from the inside, but rather is motivated by external rewards.

Psychologist Paul Wink of Wellesley College followed teens for 50 years who exhibited a tendency for generosity in adolescence and found that giving of themselves during the teen years predicted good mental and physical health in adulthood. Giving, according to studies at the Institute of Gerontology at the University of Michigan, is more powerful than receiving in terms of reducing mortality.

Again, the act of giving releases the hormone oxytocin, which produces feelings of security and generosity, and a connection to others. Imagine an organization filled with positive hormones, essentially creating an environment primed for great things.

---

1. Conti, Vicki. *Brain Imaging Reveals Joys of Giving*. National Institute of Health. 6/22/2007

2. T Sheets. The Secret Recipe for a Winning Company Culture. 2016

## Goodness Changes Organizations

The spirit of an organization comes from the values a company professes and how they uphold those values in their attributes, rituals and behaviors. If leaders know how to make employees feel heard, understood and valued, then they not only lift spirits and increase productivity, they establish a culture that thrives on cooperation to achieve a common mission or goal. Leaders who encourage employees to share feedback in a tactful truthful manner, while accenting the tendency to be positive, strengthen relationships and encourage communication. In addition, this focus encourages teamwork.

On September 28, 2018, millions of Americans witnessed the senate judiciary committee debate regarding the nomination of Brett Kavanaugh for Justice of the Supreme Court. The bi-partisan wrangling in regard to Dr. Christine Blasey Ford's allegation of sexual assault shook the nation and increased divisiveness within the political landscape. Sadly, Congress epitomized the kind of poor leadership that is created by biased, black-and-white thinking which refuses to consider alternative points of view. Both sides continue to be entrenched in their refusal to consider the value of diverse perspectives. Senator Jeff Flake broke this deadlock of perception when he stopped to listen to victims of sexual abuse as they approached him at an elevator door. His facial expression conveyed his torment as they pleaded with him to reconsider and delay confirmation. Despite his earlier decision to vote for Judge Kavanagh without an FBI probe, he reconsidered and brokered an extension, which had previously been denied.

This event is an example of exemplary leadership, something that was so obviously missing during the hearing. Without considering that one's opinions are possibly incorrect, or in need of amendment, leaders cannot give due consideration to their employees, their constituents, their communities or their families. We lead effectively when we respect the voices of others, and don't assume we are all-knowing. A leader who assumes knowledge from a righteous perspective displays deep insecurity, stubbornness, and arrogance, which are characteristic symptoms of a dysfunctional organization.

On September 28th, our nation was given a gift: the gift of compassion, which was produced by allowing the voice of a young, courageous woman to be heard. The decision lifted the spirits of millions of viewers, as Congress recommitted itself to discerning the facts without bias.

What if we, as leaders, gave every employee a chance to be heard? What if we established a business culture that promoted the idea that everyone on our team has the respect of leadership? 60% of American workers have indicated that they would take a pay cut to work for an organization with a culture that promotes and practices empathy.[3] People will follow a leader who they respect, and in some cases, one who they come to love. Despite the tremendous emphasis on money in our culture, there is clearly something more important in our DNA. We all want to be loved, respected and valued. Leaders that practice empathy and compassion, create teams that exhibit exceptional creativity, productivity and profitability.

---

3. Inc. Want to Double Your Employees' Loyalty? Science Says Provide These 3 Things. Marissa Levin. August 15, 2016

# 2.

## Integrity: Motivated by Goodness not Status or Image

*"The soul is dyed the color of its thoughts. Think only on those things that are in line with your principles and can bear the light of day. The content of your character is your choice. Day by day, what you do is who you become. Your integrity is your destiny—it is the light that guides your way."*

—Heraclitus

CAN YOU IMAGINE BEING a four-year-old child, playing with your three siblings and suddenly you hear a scream from your mother in the kitchen as she drops the phone to the floor? Paul's father had suffered a massive heart attack, causing his mother to fall into a deep depression. She began to drink heavily, and out of desperation married an angry, belligerent man who beat all her children except Paul's youngest sister. The three boys suffered unbelievable abuse, but all the children, except Paul and his sister, were able to grow into adulthood with some semblance of self-esteem. Research has shown that a child needs one reasonable, caring, consistent adult in his or her life to become a stable, healthy individual. For Paul, that individual was his uncle, a man that was courageous enough to confront Paul's stepfather. Paul had not spoken to his stepfather since Paul's mother's early death at age 54 from sclerosis of the liver.

Paul's stepfather is currently in a nursing home facing the end of his life. He has repeatedly demanded that the nurses there contact his stepchildren to have them visit him. Only Paul has made the journey, going every Sunday for several weeks, sometimes alone, and sometimes with his fourteen-year-old son. His siblings refuse to see their stepfather, as they have never forgiven him for the trauma he inflicted on the entire family.

As a psychologist, I am always interested in understanding how people overcome tragedy and live with a strong sense of integrity. Integrity and character are intimately connected. I asked Paul one day why he visits the man who caused him so much pain? What would you, the reader, do? Would you overcome your pain to do the right thing or would you, as Paul's siblings have done, hold your resentment so close that you could not bear ever seeing this individual?

Paul's response to my question: "I can't bear the thought of him dying alone. I know he was evil, but I also know his father was the same; brutality was a way of life for him. Don't get me wrong, I don't love him. But I also don't hate him. I can't maintain my view of myself by punishing him when he is begging for contact. Soon it will be over and I will be at peace with myself."

Outdoing his siblings does not motivate Paul's actions, he doesn't even tell them when he visits their stepfather. He is motivated by empathy, putting himself in his stepfather's shoes, and by a deep desire to maintain his integrity. He is now in his early 50s, a partner in a mortgage company that has been very successful for many years. Why? Because he is always truthful and caring, and because he takes both pleasure and pride in servicing his clients. They experience his integrity.

## A Few Facts

CFOs were asked in a survey which qualities, other than technical expertise, they value most in selecting leaders for their organizations. They chose integrity as the most important variable, with communication skills being rated second. Honesty is the platform on which integrity rests, and in the workplace an honest leader creates trust and a willingness to sacrifice for the common good. Employees will actually agree to reduce their pay and their bonuses if they work for a leader with integrity, exemplified by his or her honesty. If a company is in financial trouble, and leaders are transparent, then employees will make the sacrifice of less income to remain in a corporate model where respect is reciprocal between leadership and employee.

The Great Place to Work Institute found through their surveys that a culture of integrity within a corporation leads to lower turnover rates, higher morale, higher earnings and increases in share prices.

In essence, high earnings are a product of a culture of integrity.

## Early Origins: Greed vs. Integrity

When I was eight years old I was the only player my age on my little league baseball team. My coach, looking in my direction in the final inning of a close game, shouted "Semicola, Coca-Cola, Pepsi cola, get up to bat!" I was traumatized and frozen at the plate as I took three call strikes and returned to the dugout humiliated in front of my older peers. As has been proven by trauma experts, we don't forget the particulars of the humiliation but instead forget the peripheral elements. I don't know where this took place. I don't remember the day or the temperature, but I remember every word he said. I can tell you his name, what he was wearing, and I can describe his physical stature accurately.

As players and parents left the field I remained in the stands feeling sorry for myself, calling myself names and making the situation worse minute by minute. As I started to rise I noticed a little black pouch beside my feet. I picked it up, moved the zipper and found thirty dollars in cash. Suddenly, my mood changed from one of despair to one of elation. Oh, my God, I had thirty dollars!

## Being completely honest, what would you, as an eight-year-old child, have done with the money?

Thirty dollars was enough to buy the best glove and the best bat at the local sports store. I lived in a small blue-collar town, and the main street where my parents owned a furniture store was only a short distance away from the ball field. Of course I had to pass the sporting goods store on the way to the field.

I looked inside the store window, hiding the small purse in my back pocket and started to dream of owning the glove in the window. After all, I deserved something for being humiliated by the coach. And why had I been saddled with such a long name, one so difficult for everyone to pronounce? Didn't I deserve something for all I had been through? But for some reason I could not enter the store. I began to feel guilty. What if this was an older woman's purse? What if she needed the money for food, or for her family? I was in a quandary. This was the first time in my life that I'd had to wrestle with the choice of being greedy or taking a higher road and being honest.

I just couldn't enter the store once I started thinking about the older woman that might own this purse. I assumed it was an older woman because I had seen my grandmothers with similar purses. After a few minutes of ambivalence I walked a few blocks down to my parents' store. I walked inside and handed my dad the money, and I can still see the pride on his face that his son had done the right thing.

He immediately called the local radio station and they aired the story, looking for the owner of the purse. Ironically, it was the purse of an elderly lady, and she wrote me a beautiful letter thanking me for my honesty. So, no glove, and no bat, but I did experience a positive brain change caused by the development of integrity. I still remember that day vividly, though I'm not so sure I would have remembered the glove or bat for very long.

## A Cultural Crisis

The story above is an example of how integrity becomes part of a person's character. Somewhere inside me I knew what I should do because I had been taught at a young age that character matters more than money. I had been taught to look beyond my own needs to determine the needs of others. If we don't grow up in a family that values integrity, then we don't develop that aspect of our character. If your parents tell you to lie about your age to reduce the movie theatre ticket price, then you begin to see how you can manipulate the truth for your personal gain. These small examples set the stage for adult behavior.

I have listened to many people discuss their fears during the course of my career, but recently the nature of those fears seems to have changed. For the first time in my many years, people are talking about their fears concerning our current society. Many Americans believe this is the worst time in our history. More than at any time in my life I hear people longing for leaders with integrity, with the courage to speak up, even when their pocket books may be affected. 80% of companies are now using assessment surveys, with tests to determine one's integrity becoming increasingly popular. Employers consistently rate honesty and integrity as the most important characteristic for an employee. Wasn't there a time when we didn't have to test for integrity? Wasn't integrity the foundation of our culture?

Interestingly, certified B corporations, those that create value for their employees, the local community and the environment, are growing rapidly. There are now 2,655 B Corporations in 60 countries. Companies like Patagonia, Etsy, and Ben and Jerry's have adopted the B Corporation model, making the environment and social issues priorities in their business model. Surveys show that workers want to work for socially aware companies, and will sacrifice income to be part of a meaningful venture. B corps are demonstrating that a company can maintain integrity and also make a profit; in fact, having societal objectives makes a company more attractive to consumers, as well as to potential employees.[1]

## Gratitude is the opposite of greed

But how can we be grateful if we grow up in a society that values money and appearance more that relationships and character? How can we be grateful if we work for an organization that applauds performance and ignores character?

Leading indicators dictate the behavior of a company; lagging indicators are the scorecard of results: market share, profits—all indicators of financial success. Lagging indicators can create bad behavior if

---

1. bcorporation.net

companies are geared to meet 'numbers' while sacrificing ethics, honesty, and authenticity. Interestingly, companies that adhere to AIE leadership have better lagging indicators, and better financial results.

As one of my clients who works in sales always says, "You're only valued for the points you put on the board today." Many simply adapt to such an environment and come to believe that working in the business world is not a place to feel valued and respected.

Our friend Paul, however, was not one who would accept leadership without integrity. Even though he didn't grow up in a family that taught him to be ethical and honest, he sought out those who possessed ethical qualities. He realized early that the behavior of his stepfather was not to be emulated. He sought out mentors early in life—teachers, coaches, and ministers who functioned with integrity. He took to those who showed him kindness, respect and were willing to teach him how to navigate the complexities of life.

Rather than living with resentment for his past, Paul made the decision to be grateful for the opportunities he had in the present. Most of us grow up with scars; however, they are not necessarily our fate. We must often abandon much of what we learned early in life in order to become more effective, compassionate leaders who show respect for others and in turn garner respect for ourselves from those we lead. We all have goodness within us, but we often need others to help us release this goodness when it is smothered by hurts from the past. Sometimes we learn what to do by witnessing what not to do, remembering how certain negative behavior affected us.

The first leaders in our lives are our parents: if they teach and model integrity, then we grow with integrity; if they do not know how to do so, then we must seek others who can teach, mentor and guide us. We live and work in a time when integrity is far from a given among leaders. One of every five leaders is said to be toxic; some studies say it is closer to three out of every 10. Regardless of your past, try to be a leader with integrity in the present. Search out those who lead with integrity, study their behaviors, their attitudes and most of all the way they relate to others, in good times and in bad times.

Always remember that without integrity we weaken our body and mind and lose the respect of those close to us.

# 3.

## Humility: Leading from the Bottom Up not Top Down

*"No matter how good you think you are as a leader, my goodness, the people around you will have all kinds of ideas for how you can get better. So for me, the most fundamental thing about leadership is to have the humility to continue to get feedback and to try to get better—because your job is to try to help everybody else get better."*

—Jim Yong Kim

IMAGINE HOW YOU WOULD feel if your company was just bought by a giant in the business world and their headquarters are on the other side of the country. You have worked for your current company for over 20 years, you are happy, you admire your colleagues and your work continues to be challenging and interesting. Now your world is upside down. You have new management, they are not so friendly, they are more bottom-line than any of the managers for whom you have ever worked. They are not particularly interested in getting to know you as an individual, and they have made it clear that those who produce will remain, and those they deem to be dead weight will be offered a package. You don't know what the package entails, you don't know if you stay if you will have to move, and

15

at age 51 you never planned on being in this position.

What would you do? Would you contact a recruiter and add your resume on LinkedIn? Would you ask questions of your new boss to see if you have a chance of surviving in this new culture? Would you move your family across the country? Would you even want to? And where would you go if you decide to leave?

This exact situation is happening to a few of my clients who work for a local company. They deeply resent the arrogance they have encountered by those now in power. Rather than being approached by the new owners, those in the smaller, more vulnerable company have been made to feel second rate.

A recent Harvard Business Review article by behavioral scientist Francesca Gino stated that 70% of 3,000 employees surveyed said they encounter barriers to asking questions at work.[1] No wonder, according to a Gallup 2017 State of the American workplace report, that 70% of American workers feel disengaged at work. Feeling disengaged and afraid to ask questions produces stress and unhappiness. The lack of humility of those in charge will reduce satisfaction in the workplace and as a result production is likely to decrease as well as the quality of the work produced.[2]

It is probably apparent to you that the takeover situation I described above could have been handled differently, even though you also realize this approach is far too common.

What if the leadership (CEO, CFO, CIO) had gathered the new group together in a town meeting style encounter, scheduled a two-hour slot where they could honestly explain their intentions, relay the appreciation

---

1. Gino, Francesca. Small Measures Liberate Employees to Contribute Their Best. Harvard Business Review. 11/2/2016

2. Gallup. State of the American Workplace Report. 2017

they have for their employees, detailing the reasons the purchase was of great interest in the first place, and also indicate the problems that must be addressed going forward. What if they had humbly acknowledged that they don't have all the answers and are willing to hear opinions of those employees who can educate leadership as to the culture, capability and product development of the organization that they had just purchased.

In essence, they would be saying, *"We need you to be part of the process. Integrating two companies won't be easy, but if we listen to each other in an open manner, we are likely to meld both worlds together, accenting each company's strengths, and hopefully to everyone's advantage."*

Such an approach would convey that the leadership does not assume that they understand the concerns of workers, nor do they know individuals well enough to make decisions.

Humility is about understanding what we do know and acknowledging what we do not know. It is about knowing who we are, what we are capable of and what is out of our realm of expertise. It is about honesty in the appraisal of ourselves and all that we do. Leaders who are naturally humble have no difficulty uttering the phrase, *I don't know.*

A CEO with whom I am familiar was interviewed on one of the national business TV stations several years ago. He was asked if his company would meet quarterly projections. His answer: *"Absolutely!"* That year his company's stock price dropped 80%. He now says it was the biggest mistake of his career. He knew his company would never reach the projected earnings but he had conditioned himself to always answer in the affirmative. He now states that he had always felt that saying *'I don't know'* was not part of his vocabulary. Now, **he deeply regrets not realizing that uncertainty is actually a friend of honesty**. There are situations, especially in the business world, which are clearly uncertain.

*"If I had been truthful in that interview, I would have saved investors and stock holders thousands if not millions of dollars. How very foolish of me!"*

**Pride and egotism are the opposite of humility.** Humility keeps us from being sidetracked by the struggle to be something we are not. When we have nothing to hide, when our ego is in check, we can ask for feedback, we can open the door to diverse opinions. The CEO above had ignored the opinions of his associates, and in fact they shuddered listening to him on national TV. They knew he had just created an unrealistic goal, which would demand more and more hours of work, all the while knowing the results would not be favorable. This type of leadership dampens the spirit of a work culture. A leader with a large ego is not one that people trust or feel close to, as they know their leader's pride will interfere with his understanding of how he is affecting those below him.

## Leading from the Bottom Up

With humility we avoid undue pride in our achievements and the equally self-defeating tendency to be deflated by accenting our faults. We arrive at a position of balance, with a real awareness of our strengths and weaknesses. From this perspective we can develop an attitude of humility. Similar to my father's instruction to engage with the man cleaning our building, we need to endorse an attitude of engagement with everyone we encounter.

**As a leader the moment you enter your building you are an influencer. If you walk past secretaries, receptionists, and cleaning personnel without speaking to them, or act like you are too busy or too important to make contact, then you will have had a profoundly negative influence. Imagine his**

**Holiness The Dalai Lama entering your building. He would be smiling, giving looks of affection, asking a few questions of those he passes, and he would be making every individual feel special.** He would be changing their brain chemistry for the better, and it would likely last throughout the day. He mentions in one of his books that if you smile and wave at passing cars, then they will likely smile and wave back. I often walk our dogs in our neighborhood. I am often dismayed that people seldom make eye contact when walking past me, and very seldom when passing in a car. So I decided to do an experiment one Sunday. I smiled and waved at every passing car, and I did the same to those passing me on foot. 90% of those I encountered responded positively. I had initiated a change—a change that I had not previously thought about, although the lack of warmth in our neighborhood had often bothered me.

As you listen to this story, how are you feeling? Would you dare to do the same as you enter your building? Happiness is contagious, and you as a leader are being observed and looked to for direction more than anyone else. Your attitude becomes your organization's attitude. **Simple human interactions change brain chemistry.** When you treat people with kindness, you produce the feel good chemicals serotonin and dopamine. When you do so you make people happy, and happy people are more creative and more productive, and they are more committed to achieving the goals of your organization.

When I began my career, I worked for a couple of Freudian psychoanalysts. I would greet patients with a friendly hello; sometimes I would bring a patient coffee or tea, making an attempt to make them feel comfortable, because they were about to reveal very personal aspects of their lives to me.

During a supervision meeting I was told that I was gratifying patients, and that I should not be bringing them coffee or tea, that I was not remaining neutral. Freud had stated in his early writing that the analyst has to be as objective in perspective as the surgeon with his knife.

Shortly after this encounter, I visited my mother. My mom left school in the seventh grade (her father believed that girls did not need to be educated and should join the work force as soon as possible to help the family financially). Nevertheless, my mother had great compassion and knew how to cultivate relationships with diverse groups of people. People talked to her about very personal issues in their lives. She made them feel comfortable, and as a result they opened their hearts to her.

When I told my mother about my supervisors' comments, she smiled and said, "Not everything you need to know about helping people is in a book." As a young intern I was videotaped meeting with a patient and was told that I was too animated, that I was moving my hands and giving gestures of approval. My supervisor actually told me to sit on my hands so I would not reveal approval.

I believe that my mother and the Dalai Lama have influenced far more lives positively than my old supervisors. Be yourself, be warm, be wise, set realistic limits, be honest, and most importantly, be humble, and your days in the office will be much happier and more profitable.

# 4.

# Happiness: Knowing How to Work and Play without Stress

*"Happiness doesn't depend on any external conditions, it is governed by our mental attitude."*

—Dale Carnegie

YES, HAPPINESS DEPENDS UPON our attitude, and even more upon how we perceive others and ourselves. When we misperceive, we are likely to experience stress and anxiety. Also, when we misperceive, we will have difficulty maintaining loving relationships. One of the greatest misperceptions in our culture is that material success will make us happy. Happy people tend to be more successful, but many successful people are quite unhappy, not knowing to connect and help their employees thrive.[1]

According to a recent Harvard study, 76% of those who say they are extremely happy give primary credit to the success of their intimate relationships. 78% of those who are extremely happy exercise at least three times a week, and 93% who are extremely happy say they are in very good health. The survey authors recommend that leaders make sure they access how employees feel

---

1. Mills.H., and Dombeck, M. Resilience: Social Support Benefits. MentalHelp.net

about their jobs, as well as invest in team members' relationships, physical, financial and overall well-being.[2] We know that success in and of itself does not make people happy, but happy people are far more likely to be successful.

The companies ranked highest in increased happiness by Forbes are Staples, Direct TV, WIPRO Technologies, Citibank, Xerox, Cognizant, Symantec, Raytheon, UPS, and Best Buy.[3]

Recently I met with an executive and his wife from one of the above companies. The core issue causing tension in their marriage was his work hours and his other business interests outside his corporate job. He resents that he does not have enough time to do more consulting, and more work at night now that they have two children. He told me he has not had a good night's sleep in twelve years. He falls asleep but wakes up thinking about his job, how to increase profits, motivate employees, create new opportunities. He is unusually critical of himself, noting mistakes he makes and believing that with his intelligence he should be able to predict certain negative outcomes and avoid them. He is a perfectionist and does not see that mistakes are part of being human, part of the learning process. He has no tolerance for being average; he must excel in everything he tries, and as a result, happiness has eluded him.

Frank is forty-five years old, handsome, articulate and very devoted to his children and wife. However, he is always uneasy when he is with them because mentally, as hard as he tries, he is really not fully present.

---

2. Mineo, Liz. Good Genes are Nice, but Joy is Better. The Harvard Gazette. 4/11/2017

3. Kauflin, Jeff. The Happiest Companies To Work For In 2018. Forbes. 12/3/2017

When he works long days he feels guilty for not spending enough time with his family. When he is with his family, he is preoccupied with all the work he left at the office.

## Performance Addiction

Performance addiction is the belief that perfecting appearance and achieving status will secure love and respect. It is an irrational belief system that originates within a person's family and is reinforced by our culture.

Performance addicts are always on the move, trying to achieve more to prove their worth. As a result they have great difficulty calming themselves, and sleep loss is usually a major problem. There is always an early story that begins this elusive quest for worth. In Frank's case, he grew up in a home where no one felt safe. His mother drank excessively and his dad suffered from depression most of his life.

Frank did not feel valued for simply being himself. As a star athlete, he received praise from many outside his family, thus the addiction to achievement as the only way to feel worthy began quite early in his life. Now, as an adult, he can't relax, as performance addiction is insatiable. He can't perfect his world, and thus happiness remains elusive.

I have worked with many clients like Frank. Slowly but surely, they realize that love and respect cannot be obtained simply by achievement and appearance. In real estate they say the answer to success is location, location, location; happiness, as the Harvard survey indicates, is obtained by connection, connection, connection!

As a therapist, I have led communication and leadership groups for over 30 years. Within such groups one's resume, title, or net worth means nothing. People are assessed for their value based on how they relate to others in real time. Do they listen attentively? Do they possess humility? Do they tell the truth? Are they arrogant? Are they warm, caring, empathic? These are the attributes that make a difference in this setting, and they are the attributes that make a difference in all aspects of life. Most importantly, when one relates with empathy and compassion, brain chemicals are produced that make us happy. So the elusive chase for happiness through possessions, titles and bank accounts proves to be a misguided attempt to make up for childhood hurts that were never resolved.

We don't resolve old hurts by looking forward; we must look behind us to locate the experiences in life that led us to believe that we were not worthy.

One of my clients, a retired former CEO, spent his life believing that the only way for him to be valued by others was to build his company to be one of the most respected in his state. After years of 80 hour weeks and constant travel, he was shocked into awareness by his wife's lingering battle with ovarian cancer. Her last wish before she died was for him to *tell each of their children that he loves them each time he sees them, and to remember to hug them.*

Ralph fell into a deep depression after her death, and for the first time in his adult life stopped going to work. He began to realize the value of his wife, how much he had loved her, but also how little attention he had paid her. "I am old school, I thought she was the mother, I was the worker. She did the kids' homework, went to all four of their games while I was on the road doing what I thought was right."

Ralph came to me confused, guilty and very reluctant to follow through with his wife's wishes. It wasn't that he didn't love his children, but he had never been hugged, nor had he heard the words 'I love you' himself. In our group sessions he labeled himself Mr.

Black-and-White, knowing he has always had difficulty understanding the emotional world.

Ralph would interrupt sessions, had great difficulty during even the shortest periods of silence, and to his credit, absorbed the feedback of other members. Every week he seemed to improve; over time he became a much better listener and he communicated in a more open manner. As his heart slowly mended, his natural goodness began to emerge. He became a champion for family involvement. He recently convinced a woman to visit her abusive father who was at the end of his life. She has thanked him many times as she knows she would have regretted missing the opportunity to speak to her father one last time.

Interestingly, the woman that Ralph had the most difficulty with was also a performance addict. She was the president of a legal team who admits wishing that she never had children, although she wishes she felt differently.

Lorraine affects Ralph because he is trying so hard to be a good father and a loving grandfather. He realizes his mistakes and he has trouble understanding her lack of interest in her children. Often times, when we encounter someone we feel uneasy with, it is because they are holding a mirror up to us. Ralph's reaction to Lorraine is strong, not only because he has finally been able to hug his children and tell them that he loves them, but because she reminds him of how self-absorbed he was during the critical years of his children's development and how he himself was too self-absorbed to give to his wife the way he has learned to give to others today.

So often, when very driven people recover the goodness that has been submerged, they experience a depth of joy and happiness that they have never known. A recent U.S. study from the University of Rochester indicates that happiness is produced by loving relationships, personal growth and community contributions. As confirmed by previous research, wealth, fame and image do little or nothing to boost a person's mood, and in fact significantly contribute to ill-health.

Human beings will always feel happy when they know that they are loved for who they are, not just for what they do. In the final analysis, if you don't have good character, then you are unlikely to be able to experience joy with consistency.

# 5.

## Tolerance: Adjusting Your Temperature Accordingly

*"I have learned silence from the talkative, tolerance
from the intolerant, and kindness from the unkind;
yet strangely, I am ungrateful to these teachers."*

—Kahlil Gibran

OVER THE PAST FEW years we have witnessed many in power speaking and acting in a manner that conveys a lack of tolerance for opinions and perspectives other than their own. Many social scientists believe we are experiencing an Age of Arrogance.

On one hand, we have corporate leaders that recognize the need for integrity, empathy and diversity; but on the other hand, we have a group of leaders who demand allegiance, insult those with opposing views, and seek vengeance on any dissenters that they cannot bring into the fold.

Intolerance for other points of view speaks to a deep sense of insecurity that is masked by aggression and attempts to belittle and demean. This type of leader, people who are self-righteous and suffer from what I call pathological certainty, will always attract angry, black-and-white thinkers. This type of leader's fragile ego does not allow him to be wrong. When questioned, he is defensive and blames others for his mistakes.

Blaming hides sadistic impulses, the desire to hurt those who are seen as threatening.

## No Dimmer Switch

Angie is a fifty-two-year-old president and principal owner of a marketing firm that services local and national politicians. She called me for a consultation. She was quite loud and entertaining on the phone. She was trying to make light of the fact that her two sons, both attorneys in her company, demanded that she see a professional to curb her temper, and learn how to address employees with more respect and less sarcasm.

As I entered the waiting room Angie jumped up and greeted me with a firm handshake. She was five feet, five inches tall and thirty to forty pounds overweight, dressed flawlessly, and obviously an extrovert. I began to take a history, as I always do during a first meeting, and I could tell that she was trying to impress me with her answers. "I live in a man's world, Doc, and I am respected. Some day, when I retire, I'm going to write a tell-all book about these cowards in congress." She also mentioned that she went out every night, and I discerned that she drank fairly heavily. I learned that her dad was an alcoholic, as were two of her brothers. She was in her second marriage, to a man she does not respect. She has had four children, and she made sure that I knew she had a home "right on the water on Martha's Vineyard." She also related that she traveled regularly to DC and stated with certainty, "No one is faithful in that city." I asked her if she had had affairs and she said, "I have never had an affair; a few one-night stands, but no affairs."

Since my schedule was full at the time, Angie and I met on four occasions over the course of five weeks when I had cancelations. During our last meeting she decided she wanted to come five days a week because she wanted to "get to the bottom of this quickly so I can sleep and work without headaches." I told her that I could not meet with her that often because my schedule was full and that it was unlikely that I would have five free hours in a single week.

Her response told me a great deal about her world, and about her character. "You can make it happen, Doc. I know you can. I want to get this done. Are you going to walk away when I'm paying cash?"

As the discussion continued she grew angrier and angrier, and when I would not agree to her demand, she stormed out of the office. Two weeks later I received this email:

*Doc: For your information I am being seen by a clinical psychologist five days a week in Cambridge. Like I said, IT CAN BE DONE! Angie*

I shared this story with a friend of mine who is an interior designer. She told me that 95% of her affluent clients act in a similar manner. In my experience, most individuals do not act this way, however such behavior is not uncommon with clients who have power, prestige and money. Credible research from (six studies on how money affects the mind, 12/20/13, Paul Piff, TEDBLOG) has demonstrated through functional MRIs that as people become more affluent they tend to become less empathic and less ethical.

## Loss of Soul

Think about Angie as a leader: a one-night stand is not an affair; her entitlement should have been accommodated; and she believed that if one has power, she can get whatever she wants. Angie had no idea that she was displaying poor character, and she was encouraging me to act likewise by suggesting that I compromise my other patients to comply with her request? Leaders with this kind of disposition believe that their needs come first, and that the smaller people below them should comply.

In my latest communication and leadership group a number of people were complaining about the lack of civility in the corporate world. One member could not understand how to leave stress at work when the demands were so great and leadership so poor. "My boss doesn't return emails or text messages yet he wants results. He demands meetings at 7:00am, or 9:00pm, whenever he feels the need, yet my needs are completely ignored." Rob, a retired CEO, commented that he would not want to be in the business world today. "So much has changed: the bottom line has become the only interest of most leaders. In my time profitability was important, but I shared our success with every employee. We had profit sharing for everyone, and people stayed with me for 20 or 30 years. It seems like that approach is gone now. I think that the behavior of leaders has deteriorated as money has become their God, and they have little awareness of what makes an organization a great place for others to work."

As we continued the discussion it became obvious that those in the room were all in similar situations, and the real work was to figure out how to cope with a dysfunctional system.

## Self-Regulation

None of us can regulate a leader who is not responsive or reasonable; we can, however, relate to those leaders without withdrawing, without feeling or showing despair, and without feeling overwhelming stress. Ask yourself what steps you believe would be necessary to maintain your physical, mental and emotional health in such situations?

**Stress is mainly produced by perception**. If one chooses to personalize the reactions of an unreasonable person, then he will experience stress. One must differentiate what is personal and what is situational. This is not easy, especially if a person has grown up with issues from authority figures that have never been resolved. Such unresolved issues can cause one to take criticism without evaluating the truth. A commitment to using empathy to discern the truth can help to ensure that one does not project sensitivities forward. Remember: blamers are experts at identifying guilty people, and they prey on those that they know they can convince to take responsibility for their mistakes. If you were taught as a child to be responsible for the behavior of others, then you will be vulnerable to leaders who unjustifiably blame and criticize.

An enormous difference exists between leaders who are excessively *driven* for status and esteem versus those who are *drawn* to do what they do for satisfaction and a sense of accomplishment. Those with purer motivation have passion for their work and for the creative enjoyment of building a team and allowing the potential of the employees with whom they work and oversee to emerge. It is critical that one knows the difference between soulful leading and egocentric overseeing.

In order to avoid being overly affected by a dysfunctional leader one needs to identify the sensitivities he retains from past experiences so that he doesn't put old faces on top of new faces.

Granted, it is hard to recognize and change our sensitivities alone; we are all too subjective. Still, one needs to be open to feedback from reasonable, compassionate people who can help us see who we truly are, not who we thought we were based on the story we wrote about ourselves early in life.

## Inner Tolerance

To reduce the stress response and remain in equilibrium one needs to develop a reasonable sense of understanding of ourselves, or a type of inner tolerance. Jay, one of the members of the group I mentioned, is a leader in a culture that is unlikely to ever value empathy, compassion and integrity. They are known for ruthless demands and unethical behavior. However, most of those in leadership roles are highly paid if their departments meet quarterly criterion. Jay has a decision to make: either he must learn how to be resilient in a noxious culture, or he must move on. Because of his negative internal story he is quite reluctant to look elsewhere, even though we all know he would be a desirable candidate for leadership positions in other companies.

Jay is frozen by his past assessment of himself. He is an example of how important it is to know oneself accurately. In time, through the consensus we as a group reach of his capabilities, he is likely to change his view, and then he will likely make the decision to move on. I have seen this journey repeated hundreds of times for those who are eager to grow and learn, and eager to shed past false ideas about themselves.

## Tolerance for Those We Love

Many workers and leaders in noxious situations bring their stress home and influence their family lives. One must take inventory during the day as to how he is or is not accumulating stress. **Remember: if you don't wind up, then you won't need to wind down.** Be diligent about the mood and behavior you bring home.

Rather than entering your home complaining that the lights were left on in the garage, or the mail has yet to be collected, be prepared to smile, to touch, and to care for those who are waiting for you. They are not your business partners, so don't expect them to act as if their bonus depends on you. Treat them with grace.

I recently did an experiment with the leaders in my group. They were complaining about not being able to wind down after work, and many expressed guilt for not being in a more positive and congenial mood, and for spreading their negative emotional state throughout their home.

"If I were to give you a magic formula for immediately reducing stress, how many of you would put that formula to the test?" I asked. They all said that they would give it a try. "Okay, here is the secret. Before entering your house, envision approaching your wife, your husband or significant other with warmth in your heart. As you imagine this possibility you will secrete oxytocin, the greatest protector against stress. As you approach him or her, kiss your loved one passionately, hug and don't let go for an entire minute. Doing so will release more oxytocin."

The women in the room couldn't wait to try this approach; the men were a bit intimated by the idea but with a little coaxing agreed.

The following week everyone except one person reported feeling less stress. As discussed earlier, a simple human interaction can make a positive brain change. The choice is yours: **Relate with love and you will be happy and more productive. Relate with tension and stress and you will be unhappy and less productive**.

# 6.

## Resilience: The Voice of Reason in Conflict

*"When we tackle obstacles, we find hidden reserves of courage and resilience we did not know we had. And it is only when we are faced with failure do we realize that these resources were always there within us. We only need to find them and move on with our lives."*

—A. P. J. Abdul Kalam

WHEN I FIRST MEET with new clients, they often assume that I am going to help them find out what is wrong with them. I, however, try to explain that I am less concerned with what they believe is wrong with them and much more concerned with bringing out the potential within them that has remained undiscovered and unutilized. Potential remains hidden either because a person has not been exposed to individuals who know how to help them discover their talents, or they are blocked from seeing their own capabilities due to unresolved hurts or both.

There are several facets of resilience, but one of the most important is how to address and resolve conflict. Angie showed her strategy of dealing with a difference of opinion by becoming aggressive, manipulative and resentful. Not unlike many of our current political leaders. It is interesting that although we are in a political climate where political parties have implicitly agreed to never cross the aisle, the American public as a whole is not as divided as our leaders.

A leader who displays resilience faces conflict and difficult circumstances and emerges as a better person. The experience changes him and his organization. Resilience helps us reach the height of the human experience. The process always begins with excellent listening. Great leaders do not react quickly or defensively. They exude calmness, not anxiety. They obtain the facts by knowing what questions to ask. They are not biased, in that they do not favor one team member over the other. They are considerate and show emotion when it is appropriate. They are not dismissive; they are engaging. They are respectful and want to hear and understand all the variables in a complicated situation.

One of my European clients, Rita, earned her MBA in Boston and now is a project manager for a Fortune 100 company. When she was hired she was assured that travel would likely be once a month and that she would rarely work on weekends. She has now worked at this company for three months. She has traveled eight of the twelve weeks, and during the first seven weeks she worked Saturday and Sunday. Her boss is like Angie: aggressive, demanding, untruthful and manipulative.

In addition to Rita's work pressure, her mother is terminally ill in Europe and she talks to her dad several times each day about her mother's condition. She sends money to her parents and to her brother, who suffers from learning difficulties. She is married, has a supportive husband and has made friends in Massachusetts, but she seldom has time to spend with them as she is exhausted by the time the weekend arrives.

Rita recently returned to her country as her mother was failing, and during the two weeks she was home, her mother died. She also had to help her father with estate affairs, reclaim a run-down home, as well as help her brother obtain additional mental health care.

Rita mentioned to me via email that she wished she was more resilient as she was feeling exhausted and weary. **I responded that resilience is not determined by how a person feels, but rather by what a person does.** Rita is unquestionably resilient: she works long hours, travels often and supports her family, all while being the object of unethical behavior on the part of her superiors.

In my experience, Rita suffers from a common conflict among women. She is reluctant to hold people to their word. She is far too tolerant of inappropriate excuses as to why her bonuses have been delayed, or why her male counterparts on her team make partner but she is delayed even though her performance reviews exceed theirs.

In our leadership group, we posed the question of why women tend to accept irrational reasons as to why they don't advance. In each case I commented that the women, except for one CFO, too easily accept consequences they do not deserve. The one woman who differed in approach has learned to assert herself without the worry of not seeming feminine. The other women clearly view assertive as aggressive. They have been taught, as one woman indicated, 'to be nice, not demanding'. This is a result of cultural and familial gender conditioning.

Effective leaders, regardless of gender, need to be assertive, not passive or aggressive. Assertive leaders who are fact oriented, who tell the truth without exaggeration or manipulation, will receive respect from all involved. In addition, leaders who lead a healthy lifestyle, exercise consistently, eat well, sleep well, and have deep connections with friends and family in their personal lives are respected as they serve as models for a healthy professional and personal lifestyle. Many studies have determined that social support, more than any other factor, correlates with resilience.[1]

Rita loves to exercise, she is an accomplished cyclist. With her busy schedule, however, in and out of hotels every week, late dinners with clients and early meetings, she misses most workouts, ends up eating late at night, and goes into the next day sleep deprived.

One of my favorite books addressing overall health is Dr. Kenneth Pelletier's book, *Sound Mind, Sound Body*.[2] Dr. Pelletier's book is based on his review of a classic study of 53 prominent individuals who represent excellent examples of optimal health. 'Prominent' is defined as being recognized by peers as being accomplished in their chosen field or business. The study involved 21 women and 30 men.

**Key findings:**

- They all had a quest for deeper meaning in life, beyond material possessions and the need to compete.

- They had clear ideas of what they wanted in life and they knew how to express their needs.

- They lived passionate lives, loved humor and valued their connections to others.

- They were empathic and compassionate, in many cases based on learning from traumatic experiences. (What today would be called Post Traumatic Growth.)

Recent research indicates that empathy forms the basis of moral reasoning, which is closely related to ethical behavior.

---

1. Mills.H., and Dombeck, M. Resilience: Social Support Benefits. MentalHelp.net

2. Pelletier.K. *Sound Mind-Sound Body*. New York: Simon and Shuster.1994

In addition, the interviews showed that working through childhood hurts was critical to adult physical and psychologic health. Each person interviewed was required to help those beyond his own family as a young person, which established a keen interest in community and nation.

This seminal study tells us that optimal leadership includes qualities that surpass the narrow objective of making money. In fact, most participants came from modest means, and although they accumulated significant wealth, it was not the driving force behind their success. As previously discussed, happiness cannot be pursued directly, rather it is obtained by having a greater purpose beyond oneself.

The pursuit for deeper meaning in one's life is important for resilience, as it allows us to see conflict in a more expansive manner. What does this conflict represent? How does this difference of opinion affect our organization? Is it large or small in terms of its overall impact?

One of my clients who works in the pharmaceutical industry is a key example. He couldn't sleep at night because he knew his colleagues were lying to investors. In the short term his public comments increased his company's stock price (the narrow goal had been attained), but in the long term he knew that he was promoting a drug that would have significant side effects that had yet to be revealed.

All leaders face such difficult circumstances, but if you give up your integrity, you will undermine your natural tendency toward resilience. Damage your integrity time and time again, and you will lose your self-esteem, which is a key marker of well-being.

# 7.

# Soulful Listeners:
# An Aware Organization

*"Most people do not listen with the intent to understand; they listen with the intent to reply."*

—Stephen R. Covey

ALL HUMAN BEINGS WANT to be listened to and understood. Steven Covey's comment refers to those who half-listen, those whose insecurity or inability to calm themselves causes them to be preoccupied and unable to concentrate and focus. Ego driven listening creates resentment, and the person often feels judged as unworthy of attention. When a leader consistently interrupts, it reverberates throughout his organization. Employees talk about him in derogatory ways and will likely undermine him because they feel that he undermines them.

## Constructive Listening

Soulful listeners focus on what is said, and also what is not said. They pay attention to body language and emotional tone, and they acquire information in a thoughtful, comprehensive manner. They not only listen to a voice, they attend to all aspects of how a particular individual is communicating.

**Studies indicate that people remember half of**

**what they hear only a few minutes later.** Great leaders far exceed this trend; they know how to be present and, as a result of their exceptional concentration, they create an environment of trust. Without empathic listening, trust will evaporate. Empathic listening focuses on the uniqueness of the other person. Empathic listening focuses on affect; the emotion behind the sentences is key to understanding the intent, motivation, fear, anxiety and worry of an employee. When we only listen to content and ignore emotion, we miss critical information. An employee who says 'Yes I can finish that report by Monday' with his head down and his voice quivering needs to have his emotions addressed. For instance, 'I hear anxiety in your voice; can you tell me what worries you about the task?' This open-ended question conveys that you are listening, and that you want to understand whatever might be in the way of your employee performing. If emotion in this case were ignored, then your employee might walk away with even more anxiety after receiving no understanding or help in completing the task.

Further, empathic listening produces oxytocin, making people feel more generous, trustworthy and compassionate.[1]

## Oxytocin

- Reduces Anxiety
- Reduces Cortisol
- Promotes Calm
- Reduces Addictive Craving

---

1. Barraza,J. and Zak.P. *Empathy toward Strangers Triggers Oxytocin Release and Subsequent Generosity.* Values, Empathy, and Fairness across Social Barriers: Ann.N.Y. Acad.Sci. 1167: 182-189 (2009). New York Academy of Sciences.

**New Studies**

- Oyxtocin Nasal Spray for fathers who have difficulty bonding with babies—**FATHERS MORE IN TUNE WITH BABY**
- Lessens addictive cravings
- Blocks Pain

**Oxytocin is being used as a treatment for Autism.**

## Biased Listening

Self-interest interferes with accurate listening. People will usually sense when one's ego is in over-drive. They will likely know when a leader needs their performance to lift his self-esteem. The more one listens from an egocentric position, the more likely his employees will know he needs their performance to enhance his personal worth, and they will resist. They will know this is not a reciprocal process; it is a one-way street in the leader's interest, not theirs.

## Projective Listening

Leaders who are trying to manipulate others to fulfill their own needs rather than for the benefit of the organization listen with little attention to the needs or concerns of employees. They hear a word or a phrase that allows them to jump in and push their agenda. For instance, a leader who is trying to get a team to work weekends is approached about the team being exhausted as they just returned from a week of travel and want to be with their families on Saturday. Rather than responding to the request, the project manager goes off on a monolog about commitment and dedication to the company. This effort to induce guilt will work only with the truly guilty, but not with those who are able to set limits and see clearly that they are being manipulated. Trust is broken and team spirit is compromised. The message is clear: 'I don't care about you; I care only about the bottom line and what I want.'

## Prejudicial Listening

Biases, just like self-interests, interfere with empathic listening. Some years ago, I worked for a small medical group where five of us were in leadership roles. Three of the four physicians were going through divorces that year. As we expanded, we needed to hire an additional receptionist. Several candidates were interviewed, and I was told that a particular woman was the choice of the doctors, so I came in early one morning to interview the desired candidate. As I approached the waiting room, I saw a young, very attractive woman with a broad smile standing up to greet me. She was very funny, entertaining and affable. However, her resume was poorly written, she had little experience and had no idea of what was required of her. Nevertheless, my colleagues outvoted me and she was hired. As time went on we all realized we were not getting messages on time, billing was chronically late, patients were complaining about her not being at her desk to take information, and so on.

The underlying reason that this young woman was hired was that my colleagues found her attractive at a time when they themselves were suffering through the arduous process of divorce. When our emotions rule our decisions, even the brightest of the bright are blinded.

## My Problem is Your Problem

Not long ago I added Mary, a woman in her mid-fifties, to one of my communication and leadership groups.

Mary was asked by another member what made her decide to join the group. "My husband and I own a small business. Two of our major accounts have decreased, and money has become a problem. Recently, my husband acknowledged not being able to limit his drinking, and he told me that he has been hiding nips and drinking more and more once I go to bed." Sara, a small business owner herself, immediately chimed in: "He'll never stop. I went through this with my ex-husband. Get him out of the business and out of your life before he ruins everything. Trust me; I've been there." Obviously, Sara was projecting her experience onto Mary. Interestingly, Mary smiled after Sara's intense warning. "I have no intention of leaving my husband. He is a good man, a good father and he is getting help from a psychologist experienced with business owners who turn to alcohol when the pressure of business and family mounts. We have one son in a private college, another son to be entering college in September, so he and I have been overly worried about the future. I am here to learn how to express more directly; I have always kept things to myself and I know we both need to open up more and find better ways to cope." As the discussion in-group continued, Sara apologized. "I did what Doc C always warns about—identifying instead of understanding. I just assumed we had a similar experience without slowing down and understanding how your situation is different than mine. Lesson learned."

When we slow down and stop projecting a story of our own making onto another, we find common ground. Our biases must be recognized and hopefully altered so that we can see clearly and objectively. As discussed earlier, overly quick reactions are usually accompanied by distortions and biases. Heated emotions re-affirm biases, confirming what we want to see. Empathic discussions open doors, increase connections and build cultures based on truthfulness and integrity.

# 8.

## Proactive Learners: Learning from Diverse Sources

*"The illiterate of the 21ˢᵗ century will not be those who cannot read and write, but those who cannot learn, unlearn, and relearn."*

—Alvin Toffler

PROACTIVE LEARNERS ARE INDIVIDUALS who want to learn from as many sources as possible. They do not rule out learning from any individual they hire, or any individual they encounter. As my earlier story indicated, I learned from the man cleaning the floors where my office was located. Arrogant leaders think that only those of particular status are worth encountering. Openhearted learners have acquired wisdom from parents, coaches, religious figures, and all those who can impart insight in various aspects of life.

Leaders who are open to workplace diversity also realize that their companies will profit if they themselves are willing to accept alternative points of view from a variety of employee cultures and backgrounds. A report by McKinsey in 2015 of 366 public companies found that those in the top quarter for racial and ethnic diversity in management had financial outcomes 35% above the industry mean. Companies in the top quarter for gender diversity were 15% more likely to have financial outcomes above the industry mean. Learning from a diverse workforce brings new insights, new opinions, while creating a culture of acceptance.[1]

Not long ago I was interviewed on a radio program where religion became a topic as the host of the show was commenting on the Middle East and the atrocities committed in the name of religion. At one point she asked me if I identified with any particular religion. I commented that I identify with Christianity, Judaism and Buddhism. She became a bit irritated and told me I cannot believe in all three. I was somewhat perplexed until she revealed her ardent devotion to her religion. Her black and white thinking became evident as she appeared quite threatened by the idea that a person could learn from several religions, ultimately choosing aspects of each that seem meaningful.

When we are growing up we come to believe certain things about ourselves and others based on what we are told, and as well as learning from experiences we had with the authority figures in our lives. I believe that as adults we are responsible to examine those early beliefs about ourselves and about others, and search for objective truth.

Much has been said in recent years about how the brain becomes hard-wired early in life. Neuroscientists, however, have proven that we are actually soft-wired. We can change our brain's orientation through a quest for the truth. We must un-learn biases that we have accumulated and substitute those inaccurate ideas with the facts.

Proactive learners are not satisfied with anything but the truth. His Holiness the Dalai Lama invited scientists of all disciplines to Dharamsala, India to discuss

---

1. Hunt.V, Layton.D., Prince.S. *Why Diversity Matters*. McKinsey and Company 1/2015

any new findings about human nature, brain science and overall well-being. At one point in the discussion a journalist asked him how, if he desires to learn from science, he could still support the idea of reincarnation. He asked the journalist if he could prove this phenomenon is false. Of course the answer was no. The Dalai Lama then said that as soon as someone could prove it did not exist, then he would rewrite the ancient texts of Tibetan Buddhism. This experience is an example of open-minded fact finding. The Dalai Lama and Desmond Tutu are leaders of different religions, yet they are very close friends, eager to learn from each other. They acknowledge that they love each other and even kid each other about the aspects of their religions that they find to be irrational. Their differences are theoretically clear, but their goals of peace and compassion for all are more important to each of them than their particular theology.

A proactive learner has an open heart and an open mind. He expects to continue learning throughout his lifetime. He expects to revise theories as new learning takes place. He is not enamored with one way of thinking, or one way of leading. He adjusts and recalculates according to new knowledge.

When I was doing my post doctorate internship I was assigned to a forty-year-old addict who was living on the street. One day he asked me what would happen if he hit bottom. I responded, "If you hit bottom, don't worry, you will come up." Several years had passed since I'd last seen John, and one late night, during a torrid snowstorm, I went out to get groceries for my family fearing stores would be closed the next day. As I approached the checkout line I heard a voice from an aisle several feet away from me. It was John. "Hey Doc, you were the one who told me if I hit bottom I would come up. Guess what? You were wrong. When you hit bottom, you can slide sideways." I never uttered those words to anyone again.

That evening I learned to be careful with my words, to not make statements I could not factually support. John provided a learning experience for me that I did not expect. But he taught me a lesson I have never forgotten: **When you don't have an answer, don't give one.**

The best teachers I have ever had have been my clients and/or children. Children force us as parents to readdress our own childhood, adolescence and early adulthood. Every phase they go through sends us back in time. If we are willing, we have an opportunity to unlearn certain lessons of our young lives that left us with biased thinking.

I have worked with people from different backgrounds, different cultures, different countries and different religions. A few years ago I was working with an Iranian client who asked me if I knew anything about Islam. I answered honestly that I knew very little about her religion but was willing to learn. That summer I read the English version of the Koran. I was actually surprised by the content, as many of the stories were familiar to me from the Old Testament. Over time she taught me and I taught her; we were both willing to put what we had heard about each other's culture and religion aside while we readjusted our perceptions.

**When we are willing to discard old ideas to accommodate new information, we grow**. As leaders we must be open to what we do not know, and in many instances what we need to learn. One of my clients, a CEO of a fairly large company, recently told me that few of his employees know that he is an atheist. He is scientific in his thinking and cannot fathom that a God exists who could allow the Holocaust, slavery and many other horrific acts of violence and torture. He has explained to me that people are prejudiced when it comes to atheism.

"They tend to think that you are unfeeling, have poor character and lack compassion and kindness." He was direct with me and he wanted to know what I thought before we continued to work together. I acknowledged that I am spiritual; I do believe that something, some entity exists beyond us. His response: "How do you know that you weren't simply conditioned as a young child to believe, and that now you are afraid to confront the irrationality of believing in anything beyond this world?" I acknowledged that I, as well, had wondered if my faith was simply the result of early conditioning. I also acknowledged that he might be right, and that I couldn't prove that what I believe is correct. After that conversation he became more at ease, and the topic seldom comes up except in jest, when he says, 'Oh my *God*' or '*Jesus*, I can't believe that happened', and we both smile.

I have learned about Islam, atheism and other ways of living simply by trying to listen attentively, by putting aside biases and by attempting to discern the truth. Isn't that our responsibility as leaders?

# 9.

# Authenticity:
# Shedding Pretense

*"Authentic Leaders are not afraid to show emotion and vulnerability as they share in the challenges with their team. Developing a solid foundation of trust with open and honest communication is critical to authentic leadership."*

—Farshad Asl

THE HARVARD BUSINESS REVIEW, along with several other key business schools, have placed great emphasis on authenticity as being one of the most important ingredients in successful leadership. Courses in authentic leadership are in demand at most business schools and many companies are now offering authenticity training.

A Gallup poll in 2013 indicated that just 13% of employees were engaged at work, and only one out of eight was committed to their work.[1] Further studies found that trust in business leaders was at all time low, with many expecting leaders to rarely tell the truth. It is estimated that the cost of unethical behavior, such as employee fraud, costs firms $600 billion dollars a year, which in turn costs employers 20% of every dollar

---

1. Crabtree, S. Worldwide, 13% of Employees Are Engaged at Work. Gallup. 10/8/2013

earned. Fraud has grown by 50% since 1996. Interestingly, employees surveyed indicated that if managers were better role models, then unethical behavior organization-wide would diminish.[2]

Authenticity requires courage, as one is visible during his successes and during his mistakes and failures. This exposure is very important for building a culture that values honest expression.

Authentic leaders have little interest in pretense. They are the same person at work and at home. Being genuine is a quality they value. They understand the amount of energy that is expended unnecessarily by pretending to be someone other than oneself. Authenticity attracts, as it lessens the performance addict's need to perform flawlessly. Those in a realistic culture expect mistakes to be made in the process of learning.

Genuine leadership gives employees the chance to relax and to focus, and thus allows them to be at their creative best. Authenticity creates inner calm, which increases potential as well as being a positive model for others in the organization.

Companies are increasingly providing integrity, empathy and authenticity training. This trend originated from the disappointment in unethical authority figures throughout society. The cynicism that the public holds toward leaders in business and government is growing steadily, and **the need for bright, honest, ethical leaders is greater than ever.**

## The Blame Game

One of the worst qualities a leader can possess is the tendency to blame others for his shortcomings.

---

2. Mhlanga, L. *Trust at an all-time low in global institutions.* The Standard. 2/5/2017

Blaming and dodging responsibility is now the norm in politics, and the Me Too movement has also shown how pervasive denial can be from those in power. Leaders from University presidents to TV anchors to corporate CEOs have been called down and ostracized for abusive behavior. Studies have indicated that ethical behavior erodes over time; small ethical violations become large ones as time moves forward. Interestingly, a business culture that accents ethical behavior raises awareness and prompts an increase in moral judgments.

So what are the causes of such immoral behavior? How do capable people emerge with a perspective that power allows them to do whatever they desire at any given moment? A young couple I have been treating came into a session arguing about the husband Rob's behavior with their son. The dad asked his son to lie about his age to get into an amusement park for less money than his age would require. A little transgression starts the slippery slope. We begin to access which behaviors are appropriate early in life. If this boy is told that it is okay to lie to the man selling tickets, then why wouldn't he think he shouldn't steal a pen from a friend, or copy a friend's homework assignment? Maybe the boy's mother will compensate for her husband bending the rules. Hopefully that will be the case. What was most striking about this minor affront was that the husband saw nothing wrong with his behavior. He immediately blamed his wife for being too uptight. The father's blaming is equally as destructive for the child to witness as his lying.

Rob, the husband, is a commercial contractor, and within his work world he believes everybody lies. He tells his wife she trusts too easily. This may be true as she trusts his word when it is clear to me that he is shading the truth. Rob brags about the markup of certain materials, and in large projects how they frequently go unchecked, for there is so much to inventory in the construction of large buildings.

I don't find Rob to be very different than many business owners. Certainly, many are ethical and honest; however Rob uses the peer influence rationale and the idea that no one will find out anyway to justify his dishonesty and/or lack of authenticity. "We all do it; its part of the game. If you don't take care of yourself, no one else will, and most of the time no one checks." He has set the example for his employees, and for his son. Be shrewd; be smart, if you're caught, never admit you did anything wrong. Just keep spinning your story.

Rob's behavior as president of a company, despite his assertion that he doesn't take his business perspective home after work, is the same at home as it is at work. On a Friday night, after a long week, he texts his wife to say that he is going for one drink with his accounting team to go over financials, and that he will soon be home for dinner. He arrives home at 10:15pm, slurring his words, and is furious that his wife was upset when all he was doing was relaxing for a few hours.

## Causes of Lack of Ethics

Studies by the Human Resource Institute have found that the main reasons for unethical behavior in the corporate world is pressure to meet unreasonable objectives and the desire for career advancement and to protect one's job security, in that order. Other studies by the same organization have noted that cynicism, low morale and the absence of consequences are also contributors to unethical behavior.[3]

---

3. The Hidden Costs of Unethical Behavior. Josephson Institute Reports. 2005

Yet some individuals, despite difficult circumstances, still remain authentic and true to themselves? Just like Rob, **business ethics begin with personal ethics**. Every organization has a culture that either supports ethical behavior or does not pay attention to morality in general. Rob is the leader and employees follow leaders and leaders establish a business culture. When leaders make continual efforts to exemplify honesty, transparency and clarity as to what is expected of everyone, then the culture benefits.

Recently, I consulted with a medical practice where it was determined that money was missing on a regular basis. It was initially suspected that a receptionist, a secretary or someone low on the totem pole was the culprit. As it turned out, an older physician, father to a female doctor in the practice, was the person taking the money. He actually had the billing person in the office change billing sheets from patients his daughter was treating, and place those under his name, so he would get the revenue she earned unbeknownst to her. In addition, he was writing checks for large amounts and not reporting the money he took to the book-keeper. When a consulting accountant discovered his behavior, he denied his actions and blamed the billing person in the office.

Psychologists have been studying the development of moral behavior for years. It begins in the home and then it is transferred into society. All children lie early in life, and depending on the response, they either develop a sound moral conscience or not. When a child is humiliated and aggressively scolded for his actions, he will mostly remember the humiliation and not the offense, he will conform initially out of fear, and then likely rebel later out of resentment.

If one engages a child with empathy and reasonable limits, the child's lying then becomes a teaching opportunity. Children, not unlike employees, will open up if provided the security to speak. A parent or a leader is not being overly permissive, and at the same time he is not minimizing the effects of lying. His tone conveys a sense of importance to the interaction. He tries to help the child (or employee) understand how lying affects others, thus evoking and encouraging his empathy. The development of empathy makes a child, or an adult, consider the impact of his actions on other human beings. Leaders can create an empathic culture at home and in the work world.

## The Sinister Side of Authenticity

One of the mistakes ethical organizations make is the assumption that ethics can be incorporated into a culture by awareness and training alone. This is true for many, however **certain individuals will always be toxic to your organization**. Narcissistic personalities, for instance, believe that they are right and will blame others for their inappropriate actions regardless of the facts. Individuals of this nature need to be identified early so that they do not become the leaders of a negative culture within your organization. These personalities are often bright, charming and calculating. They know how to influence people and they appear to be quite genuine. Individuals with deviant consciences often present themselves as authentic, **they believe what they believe**. Authenticity means being yourself; narcissistic personalities are not necessarily originating from purposeful pretense, nevertheless their behavior is most often unhealthy and unlikely to change.

# 10.

# Beyond the Surface:
# Inspire Through Empathy

*"Empathy is the only human superpower—it can shrink distance, cut through social and power hierarchies, transcend differences, and provoke political and social change."*

—Elizabeth Thomas

EMPATHY IS THE CAPACITY to understand and respond to the unique experiences of another. It is part of our genetic endowment; it leads us to acts of altruism and generosity. **I whole-heartedly believe that empathy, more than any other quality, is the most critical element in building and maintaining a healthy personal and professional life.** Empathy teaches us who to get close to and who to remain distant from; it is a protective assessment tool that we are given at birth. Empathy needs to be developed however; if we don't practice being empathic, it atrophies and remains dormant.

Empathic leaders encourage their employees to expand their empathic range. A work culture that focuses on emotional intelligence with empathy as the foundation not only increases employee happiness but also significantly increases profit margins.

Rutgers professor Cary Cherniss, in her article "The Business Case for Emotional Intelligence," lists 19 studies that determined the profitability of emotional intelligence. She cites examples as varied as the US Air Force, 300 top-level executives from 15 global companies, to L'Oreal, Met Life and American Express, as well as a large food and beverage company and a manufacturing plant.

One of the particular noteworthy studies involved 515 senior executives accessed by the search firm Egon Zehnder International. Emotional intelligence was a better predictor of success than either relevant previous experience or high IQ.[1]

My earlier examples of his Holiness the Dalai Lama and Bishop Desmond Tutu are examples of two men with expansive ranges of empathy. They love each other because they know each other far beyond their respective titles and religious orientations. Each enjoys whomever they encounter because they know how to use empathy to find their common humanity.

## The Dark Side of Empathy

But there is a dark side of empathy. Evil leaders, politicians, and everyday people have used the power of empathy to manipulate others for their own satisfaction and gain. Empathy is an assessment tool; it allows us to determine what a person needs and wants. It allows us to look beyond the surface into the character of the person or organization we are encountering.

Think of Rob in the previous chapter. He is intelligent and quite adept at manipulating others through his use of empathy. He was using this capacity to read customers' needs and wants accurately. He knew how

---

1. Cherniss, Cary. *The Business Case for Emotional Intelligence.* Consortium for Research on Emotional Intelligence in Organizations. 199

to convince commercial real estate moguls to listen to his pitch, while padding the costs of materials and labor hours to his advantage. He knows how to use empathy to connect with others, not for humane reasons, but rather to influence others in order to satisfy his own needs. He does the same thing with his wife. He knows how to elicit her guilt and sympathy to excuse his inappropriate behavior.

## Vulnerability and Empathy

Terri is a forty-two-year-old single woman from Austin who works for a software company as a project manager. I consulted for her company, and after I gave a talk she called and asked for a meeting. She had recently been rejected in a four-year relationship with a man she cared for dearly. She was obviously depressed and felt quite alone as she had few friends in the Boston area, her family all being back in Texas.

During this time, Terri was assigned to a new boss. His reputation indicated that he was aggressive, critical and had a strong tendency to blame others for production failures. (I also had heard of this executive as the HR department that hired me had mentioned he was one of the people whose leadership style was in question.)

Terri is very bright, very attractive, as well as having a very pleasant personality. She is insightful and creative. But these abilities eroded over time as her new boss demeaned her time and time again during staff meetings. He used derogatory language and, unbeknownst to her, other employees had complained about his demeanor to HR during the past year.

I relate this story because it is a poignant example of how empathy can be used destructively rather than constructively. Terri's boss played on her guilt, and through his empathy discovered her most vulnerable places. He used this knowledge to get her to do his work, write a graduate paper for him, and sit in for him at meetings when he decided to take excessively long lunches. Remarkably, he even had her picking up his dry cleaning on her way to work.

Terri was in a bad work marriage, and very similar to actual marriages where people lose their self-worth over time as they listen to unfair criticism day after day, she lost herself and fell into a deep depression. She joined one of my leadership groups and over time began to regain her confidence as she interacted weekly with people also in the business world who valued her insight, wisdom and warm way of relating.

One day, she came into my office in tears. "I gave my letter of resignation, I can't take his criticism any longer, and I'm falling apart." I slowed down her process, asked her to call and rescind the letter until we'd had time to strategize and make a reasonable plan that was in her best interest. As Terri had gained strength through group interactions, she was able to become resilient enough to file a complaint with HR, and they ultimately acted on her behalf. I lent her my empathy so that she could assess her boss's personality accurately. Leaders who demean and humiliate employees suffer from insecurity and hidden feelings of inadequacy. Arrogance and insecurity are closely related. She began to see through my eyes, as well as those in the group, and through the eyes of her peers at work, that she was, in fact, not incompetent. Due to her circumstances in life, having just experienced the rejection of someone she loved, she was vulnerable to an authority figure reinforcing the negative self-voice she had adopted.

Ultimately, as Terry was able to expand her empathy, which was limited by her own self-doubt, she was able to see her boss realistically. She arranged for a transfer to another department, and 18 months later he was fired for behaving unreasonably to two other employees. We can see through this example the power of empathy to hurt, and the power of empathy to be protective of one's self, too. The boss used the dark side of empathy to manipulate and to exploit Terri's guilt. Ultimately, she used the positive side of empathy to understand him and to refrain from personalizing his reactions.

## Resistance to Empathy

Angelo is a very successful entrepreneur who emigrated from Europe to the US to study business in Boston. He is articulate, intelligent and relates to others warmly. He initially struggled to adapt to American culture, and has tried to fit in and become a success story. He idealizes those who have attained great success and wealth. He grew up in a very traditional household, with a demanding, controlling and dogmatic father. He joined one of my group leadership sessions to lessen stress and improve overall health. After listening to Angelo for a few sessions, it was clear that the major issue in his life was his marriage, not his business. He told us that he was puzzled as to why he could be empathic to his employees but not to his wife. He is very sensitive and felt bad about losing his temper recently with his two daughters. "I have so much on my mind when I get home. I am always thinking of how to grow the business, how to reach the top; it's not the kids' fault. Sometimes I think I'm just a bad dad, and maybe a bad husband too."

## Uncovering Empathy

How is it that we can be empathic in certain situations but not in others? Ask yourself whom you find it hardest to empathize with? Take a moment to reflect.

In Angelo's case, he has never comes to terms with his aggressive father. He never felt particularly close to him, nevertheless his father's way of leadership has been encoded in his brain. He needs to relinquish the idea that masculinity is defined by dominance. **We can try to change unhealthy ways of behaving intellectually, but unless we unlearn unhealthy perceptions and behaviors on an emotional level, old patterns will remain**. Our emotions encode behavior we have experienced in our families in a deep part of the brain. As a result, we can understand how we shouldn't act in certain ways, but when stress accumulates it is very common to fall back on old, conditioned ways of relating.

For instance, Angelo has read extensively regarding how empathy leads to better communication, higher productivity and increased profits. He has tried to emulate other corporate business models that have recognition programs designed to make employees feel validated and appreciated.

Group members, and also leaders in the business world, have pointed out to him that many companies currently have such programs, but employees can tell the difference when validation is genuine or just a new program to get them to work harder and longer. We discussed how these programs, when viewed as superficial or disingenuous, elicit more resentment than appreciation.

Angelo has a warm heart, but it is hard for him to give without fearing loss of control. He is trying to be empathic at work and at home by cognition only, not realizing that empathy requires feeling your way into another's heart and soul. It involves head and heart, not simply a cognitive process. In order to lead with empathy, one must first become aware of the resistance that blocks empathy. In Angelo's case, he cannot acknowledge that it is safe to be known, and that he can release the soft side of himself and still function competently. He, like many other leaders, needs to learn that vulnerability is a strength, not a weakness.

## Empathy and Resilience

Empathic interactions provide us with a healthy vacation from our own preoccupations. When we relate with empathy, especially if it is reciprocal, we produce feel-good chemicals like oxytocin, serotonin and dopamine that improve overall health. **The most resilient people have the capacity to experience positive emotions in the midst of stressful situations; empathy allows them to view the world with a large lens, a broader perspective, which allows them to see beyond the surface so they can still experience good in troubled times.**

Using empathy to contribute to others positively makes us happy, reduces mortality, anxiety and depression. The practice of empathy allows us to forgive ourselves for our mistakes, and we become 'imperfectly competent' and content, and as leaders we become models for resilient, high-spirited organizations.

# 11.

## Leader Deception: How Lying Affects Performance

*"You can use words to manipulate the world into delivering what you want. This is what it means to 'act politically'. This is spin. It's the specialty of unscrupulous marketers, salesmen, advertising and pickup artists, slogan-possessed utopians and psychopaths."*

—Jordan Peterson

WHEN I WAS TWENTY-EIGHT years old I bought my first home. On the way home from the closing my realtor mentioned that I wasn't friendly during the ride. I said, "You lied to me and to the seller." His response: "Everybody lies. You lie too; you're just too foolish to admit it." I have never forgotten his words because he was convinced it was normal behavior in doing business.

As I entered one of my communication and leadership groups recently I was a few minutes early. This particular group has members ranging from 45 years of age to 75 years of age. The older men were arguing as I entered, one saying, "I can't believe your company is doing business with that firm, they are known for being unethical, I was told so many lies by one of their salesman I threw him out of the building." The other responded, "You are naïve, those guys are all the same, this is business, they make us money and guess what, everybody lies."

Once again I heard that infamous line, everybody lies. Interestingly, Jeffrey Pfeffer, professor of organizational behavior at Stanford University Graduate Business School, says the average person lies a minimum of twice a day, but good leaders, according to his research, are particularly good liars. Good liars he says, become successful leaders, if success is defined by high salary and high achievement. He cites Steve Jobs' use of the 'reality distortion field,' a way of convincing people of things they do not believe in order to achieve the ultimate goal of increased profits.

Professor Pfeffer has also studied the effect of making fictitious claims of students and management personnel to those in charge. **The Pygmalion effect is the process of telling those in authority of a person's fictitious high attributes and then seeing how this false account leads supervisors to perceive employees as described, essentially purposely biasing their perceptions. This phenomenon takes place when expectations of a particular person are exaggerated to an unrealistic degree to manipulate the perception of the individual's performance.** This so-called effect has been studied extensively and subsequent research has demonstrated that when supervisors are provided false information about employees' abilities, their behavior is altered to fit the positive stereotype that was described to them. If a supervisor were told I was extremely bright and attractive, then he would begin to see those characteristics in my behavior, as well as in physical stature, as he interacted with me. Do these findings mean that if we are deceptive we can influence others to do what we want by manipulating their perspectives? Recruiters presenting candidates to businesses do this all the time, don't they?

But a specific problem exists with the Pygmalion effect. Sooner or later a person's abilities are seen accurately and those who provided the deception are also seen accurately. My realtor, I assume, knew he was unlikely to do business with me again. He might not even be a realtor by the time I purchased my next house. The first night I slept in my new home I began to feel raindrops on my forehead. Yes, the roof was leaking, even though my friendly realtor had had the entire house and the roof inspected. I later learned that the inspector was his cousin, and that they had performed this deception many times. Unfortunately, as Jordan Peterson's quote indicates, this kind of behavior has become tolerable and even given an acceptable label, **acting politically**.

Xavier Marquez of Victoria University in Wellington, New Zealand argues that if **alternative information** is not available to the public, then mythical ideas will be difficult to shift. He cites the Nazi regime as a powerful example. They had a foothold in spreading anti-Semitic attitudes as they controlled the schools and the media in Germany. As a result, the majority of Germans who lived during the Nazi regimen were influenced by the false rhetoric fueling anti-Semitism.

Cornell University professor Thomas Pepinsky spent time studying the governments of Indonesia and Malaysia to understand how authoritative regimes control the minds of those they supposedly serve. He found that they do not lie about things that can be easily checked, but rather they distort the truth through vague comments that cannot be proven or disproven. They also specialize in misdirection. They focus on providing their people with the idea that dissenters are motivated by evil intent while those in power are motivated altruistically. Professor Pepinsky also found that when alternative views are present, then manipulation becomes less effective.

This book is my attempt to present an alternative view to what I see as pervasive within our society. Americans have fewer friends than they had years ago, they are more suspicious of each other, and empathy has decreased as narcissism has increased. Race relations have worsened and the animosity toward minorities in general has increased.

How many times have employees heard during a merger that "nothing will change"? Once the lie is confirmed, the organization's soul is sacrificed and employees soon start looking elsewhere for work. Ultimately, every leader's lies add up to broken commitments, and as trust is lost, so is performance and consequently profits. A collection of studies over the last several years all indicate that employees do not have the faith that their employer will tell the truth, and we certainly acknowledge that our politicians fall into this camp as well.

It is likely that if you are reading this book you are already a leader in some capacity, or you hope to be one in the future. When I say leader, I include leaders of families and volunteer organizations, as well as leaders of businesses, educational institutions, athletic teams and drama clubs. We are all responsible for presenting an alternative view, the view of AIE leadership in all forums and in all communities, and most importantly, in our own homes.

Studies in the business world have found that if a leader lies and is successful in achieving goals and increasing profits, then employees will forget and forgive. These surveys do not have access to the soul of employees who say or act as if they forgive their untruthful leader. Do they actually trust their leader, or are they simply placating an authority figure in order to remain employed?

I find it difficult to believe that employees forgive unethical behavior unless their values condone such behavior in the first place. Increased salary or bonuses may make individuals deny or ignore the lies of a leader, but on a deeper level, when people are behind closed doors and talking with those they trust, their authentic feelings toward such leaders are usually quite different than those expressed in the presence of authority figures.

One of my clients told a story of attending a funeral for a former CFO of his company. As he was leaving, a few men were talking about the deceased, mentioning how he had few friends. One employee commented that he had one friend, Jack Daniels, and one God, money. No doubt these comments would not have been made in his presence.

# 12.

# Elusive Love:
# The Missing Ingredient

I HAVE FOUR CEOs in one of my leadership groups. Each has sacrificed everything, including mortgaging their homes, to become unusually successful. They were all going out of business at one point. They worked eighty-hour weeks, late nights, slept little and sacrificed their health in the process, either drinking or eating too much. Now they have all the money they need; they caught the elusive rabbit but one glaring aspect of their lives is missing: **it is love**.

They sacrificed their families, not intentionally, but because they were driven by false beliefs about what makes a person happy and whole. They are all intense, good people, but the ability to maintain intimacy has escaped them. They are extremely similar when it comes to the fear of being vulnerable, their fear of being known, and their fear of not being good enough. Each is an excellent example of performance addiction.

**Sidebar: Performance addiction is the belief that perfecting appearance and status will secure love and respect.**

The longest study on happiness of which I am aware has been ongoing for 75 years by Harvard professors George Valliant and Sheldon Glueck. They studied the Harvard class of 1980, and to no surprise happiness was highly correlated with "strengthening your closest relationships and taking care of yourself physically, financially and emotionally." In an updated version of the study in 2015, "75% of those extremely happy gave the highest rating to the importance of success in their intimate relationships, 77% of those extremely happy said the state of their relationship was either 'the greatest' of 'very good' versus 49% of everyone else."[1]

## A Classic Example

David's story is an example of performance addiction and the havoc this belief system can create in one's life.

David is the president and owner of a medical device distributing company. He is five feet, eight inches tall, chubby, looks older than his age, and has large, dark circles underneath his eyes. He travels extensively, and the family moved several times to accommodate his job before he owned his own company.

David married his high school sweetheart who is tiny, soft-spoken, warm and adoring. They have three children, two sons and a daughter. David was a business major at a local community college but he dropped out in the middle of his second year. His wife Ruth finished college and taught first grade for a few years before their three children were born.

David has two older brothers, both graduates of Yale with business degrees. His brothers own several

---

1. Mineo, Liz. Harvard Staff Writer. Good Genes are nice, but Joy is better. April, 11.2017

hospitals in the South. He has estranged relationships with both, although his wife communicates with her sisters-in-law.

20 years ago, David's wife called on a Sunday evening. I happened to be in my home office that night and she apologized for disturbing me and explaining that she had only intended to leave a phone message. She sounded full of panic as I listened to her quivering voice. "Our fifteen-year-old daughter Allison is acting out. She took some pills and we took her to the emergency room. I was in the ER for four hours last night. She had her stomach pumped. She is okay now; they gave us your name."

Shortly after that call we began family therapy. David made it clear that he could only attend sessions later in the evening. I worked at a local hospital at that time and agreed to see the family at 7:30pm on a Tuesday evening. I will always remember Allison's first statement: "I hate my father. I don't even want to be here, and I don't ever want to be like him. All he does is work, he's never home, he misses all my soccer games, and he doesn't even know my friends' names."

David was crushed by his daughter's comments. We met for several months and ultimately the family decided to transfer Allison to a private high school that specialized in helping young people with emotional issues. Eventually, peace was restored to the family, Allison and I went on to meet individually until she left for school, and I also continued with the couple for a time. Today, Allison is the only sibling who did not join the family business; her two brothers are now President and CFO of the family company. She now lives in Florida. She has never married but has a live-in boyfriend. She is a yoga teacher in a wellness center. She is a fitness buff, running marathons and doing triathlons. Her brothers are overweight, married with children, and for the most part live the same life as their father.

## A Concerned Prediction

Before we concluded our couple's sessions I told David that I was concerned about him. I thought that his self-care was poor, and I also thought that he would regret not spending time fostering intimacy in his marriage. He pretended that he would actually cut back on work and spend more time with Ruth, but I doubted his effort would last long.

At one point I asked him if he ever spends time alone with his wife. Interestingly, he said hardly ever. If they socialize, it is always with a group of people. He honestly admitted, "I wouldn't know what to say if it was just Ruth and me. We talk about work and managing our finances. I'm not great at the touchy-feeling stuff."

Ruth commented that she loved her husband but she could tell he rarely listened to her. "David interrupts everyone: he can't wait to talk business, and if you're not talking business, then he quickly loses interest. He is so uptight, he just can't relax. Our daughter argues with David all the time because she just wants her father to listen to her, but he either lectures or disengages."

I told David a story about a local doctor I knew who worked similarly to him, and who just had his first heart attack at age forty-two. David seemed to be affected by this story, but not enough to actually slow down and take care of himself. Ruth was pleading to remain in therapy, but David felt that Allison was okay now and that he did not have the time or the will to continue.

## Fast Forward 20 Years

One early morning I received a phone message from

a familiar voice: "Doc, it's Allison Smith; I hope you remember me. I found my dad on the floor of his home four nights ago. He'd overdosed. My mom passed away two months ago, and my dad is a mess. He can't work and has withdrawn from everything and everyone. We're hoping that you can see him again. Please call."

David and I have now met for more than two years. He has also been in one of my leadership and communication groups for a year and a half. Now that Ruth is gone, he has enormous guilt for how he seldom spent quality time with her. "I failed as a husband and as a father—lots of money and many regrets. All my life I wanted to be worthy, to match up to my Yale brothers. I made more money than both of them, but look at me: I'm fat, bald, loveless, and I taught my two sons to imitate my ways."

## Rewriting a Childhood Story

Often times when a client begins psychotherapy with me they expect that I am going to find out what is wrong with them and correct the so-called fault. In truth, I am not usually focused on what is wrong with a person, I am more interested in uncovering what has always been right with an individual that he or she has not discovered. Essentially, I am bringing forward a person's natural potentials that are hidden due to pre-conditioned thinking. We all write a story about ourselves early in life; we look into the eyes of our parents, teachers, coaches and other authority figures to understand who we are. But if the people we depend on to help us in this process are depressed, anxious, alcoholic, workaholic, critical or too demanding, then we form a false image of ourselves. What they reflect back to us is biased, but as children we cannot possibly know that what we are incorporating into our psyche about ourselves is false. Our responsibility as adults is to unlearn the original story and create a truer identity, one based on feedback from reasonable, objective, caring people in our present circumstances.

## The Story Unfolds

David grew up in a family that expected high achievement from his brothers, but not for him. His mother often spoke of him as lazy and undisciplined.

Her father had deserted her family when she was young, and she frequently compared her son to her father. It was no secret that she did not expect David to achieve as his brothers had, and he followed her expectations to a tee.

Ironically, David repeated this pattern by expecting high achievement from his sons but not from his daughter. He later realized that one of his conflicts with Allison was that she reminded him of his own family experience. One child in each family was labeled as the underdog and acted out as a result.

Countless studies over the past fifty years have demonstrated that parental expectations play a significant role in academic success. Students whose parents have high expectations obtain higher grades, higher scores on standardized tests and remain in the educational process longer than those children whose parents have low expectations.[2]

Interestingly, the same holds true for leaders and employees. When employees are expected to perform

---

2. U.S. Department of Education, Institute of Education Sciences, National Center for Education Statistics, National Household Education Surveys Program, Parent and Family Involvement in Education Survey. http://nces.ed.gov/nhes/

well, they do so. David has been able to foster this kind of environment in his company, being positive and encouraging toward his employees. However, in more intimate relationships, he has felt far too uncomfortable to be validating to his wife and, to some extent, his children. He expected great performance from his sons but remained distant from Allison once she reached puberty. It is not uncommon for fathers to become uneasy as their daughters become sexual beings. David did not know how to handle her adolescence so he worked more and interacted less with her. His sons, three and four years older than Allison, followed his line so they presented little challenge for David.

## A Goodness Breakthrough

One dynamic I am sure of is that empathy can transform a negative internal story over time in a person who has seldom had the experience of being understood. David was willing to end his life because he realized he had not adequately shown his love for Ruth. As he discussed their life together, his internal voice slowly emerged. He realized, through my empathy and group members' empathy, that Ruth loved him very much. Yes, she did want him to listen more and to be less preoccupied with work, but on the other hand she knew he was a good person with good character. She always spoke of him in glowing terms. She commented on his honesty, his loyalty to the family, and she commented on how he was the glue that kept their family together. He arranged holiday dinners, extended summer vacations, and special trips with his brothers, his parents and his family. He blocked out so much of what she had said about him because his grief did not allow him to see his behavior accurately. He also came to learn that death often comes with guilt. He had reasons to feel regretful, but not to the extent he was experiencing.

## A Leader with a Punitive Internal Voice

In my experience, many leaders in the corporate world have a punitive self-voice created early in life from family interactions. A critical inner voice, based on a lack of empathy and understanding early in life, creates an intense desire to succeed in people with performance addiction. Performance addiction is a thief of simple pleasures. It is hard to relax when you are constantly trying to put points on the board, achieving to gain an ever-fleeting sense of worth.

David is a perfectionist; like all performance addicts he has tried to perfect his way into happiness, but he is now realizing through the positive connections he has made in our group that he can be loved for simply being himself.

The group process, in particular, has shown David that he is valued not for how much money he makes, or how he looks, but for how he interacts with the other members. People love his sense of humor, they empathize with his deep regrets over his lost wife, they see how very repentant he is and they understand how deeply hurt he is for not being all he could be to her. The group experience has allowed David to release the goodness within himself that was buried by old conditioning that asserted that he did not measure up to his brothers, and that he was just a clone of his maternal grandfather.

David now knows that those old ideas are not true. It is hard for him to deny the opinions of 10 other people who have come to know him better than any other people in his life. He knows that the group members and I have made a commitment to be truthful with each other. He also knows that it is difficult to change an old story that is deeply embedded in one's mind. He has seen others discover who they are, and who they are not, as they go through the same process. He has come to realize that achievement can mask vulnerability in capable people. He has also come to realize that vulnerability can be an asset rather than a weakness. He has opened his heart, and as a result, he wants to live, and in fact, he is now living a happier life than he'd ever previously experienced. A goodness breakthrough has taken place; his authentic self has emerged!

# Conclusion: Soulful Leaders Cultivate Soulful Cultures

*"Leadership is about making others better as a result of your presence, making sure that impact lasts in your absence."*

—Sheryl Sandberg

WHAT KIND OF ORGANIZATION do you want to create? Take a few minutes before you go on reading, because your thoughts are important to consider before you hear mine.

A soulful culture, as you might expect, begins with you. Sheryl Sandberg's comment above is poignant because it emphasizes what happens in your company when you are not present. If your model of interacting is firmly implanted in the spirit of your organization, then you won't need to be present. If your employees see you as intelligent, creative, with good business sense, you will command their attention. But those qualities won't be enough to keep them invested and committed. **If you are empathic, a great listener, highly ethical with high integrity, authentic, humble yet confident, happy yet intensely serious when you need to be, then they will follow you and remain committed to your vision.** No leader can exemplify these qualities all the time, and you can't expect employees to perform perfectly either. Employees need you to display faith in yourself, and in them. You need to show them how you reach for the stars, but when you fail, you smile, adjust your reach and still try to actualize your potential.

## "We" Instead of "Me"

I grew up in a business environment. My father and mother owned a furniture store in our small, blue-collar town. Our town was often called the 'melting pot' as it was more diverse than the more affluent towns in the area. My father, after returning from World War II, worked various jobs but eventually started his own business against formidable odds.

There were already three furniture stores in town that had been in existence for many years. They had the backing of family money and could offer loans to customers, whereas my parents could not. They sold relatively low caliber furniture, so my father decided to do the opposite. He started his business by carrying more reputable furniture brands, offering no financing and with no financial backing.

My dad was the first, to my knowledge, to hire a black company to install rugs in our area. He knew his friend Onnie was the best in the business, as he would say, and despite the possibility of prejudice hurting his bottom line, my dad subcontracted Onnie for the entire 20 years he had his company. My dad didn't offer perks and benefits to employees; he offered them trust, longevity, freedom to speak and question his approach, and most importantly, he offered them lasting friendship.

## A Few Facts

Most studies indicate that the culture of a company accounts for 20% to 30% of the difference in corporate performance compared to culturally unremarkable competitors[1]. Interestingly, the top 15 best company cultures, according to *Entrepreneur* and CultureIQ, still have their original founders leading the companies.[2] Original founders tend to be more engaging, and engaged employees raise revenue 40% more than disengaged ones; they outperform the disengaged by 20% to 28% and they take 60% fewer sick days. An analysis of studies by Lolly Daskal indicates that all employees need to be engaged to feel safe, to feel that they matter and that they belong.[3]

## My Early Training

I worked for my father during my teenage years and throughout college. I used to watch him wait on customers and I was impressed with how passionate he was, and how convincing he could be about the product he was selling. I remember his words: "If you buy this sofa, it will last 20 years or more. You might have to replace the cushions—the fabric is sturdy but eventually it will wear—but the structure will never fail, mark my words!" Then he, all five feet, six inches of him, would pick up the sofa and explain how it was made, detailing the wood, the beveling, and the manner of connecting sides to the foundation. He told the truth, he was genuine, he was kind and he conveyed his intense belief in in what he was selling.

As the years passed, people would come up to me in the street and repeat his words. They would tell me that he'd been right, and that their sofa was still intact.

---

1. Coleman, John. Six Components of a Great Culture. Harvard Business Review. May 6, 2013.

2. Large–Sized Companies: The Best Company Cultures in 2017. Entrepreneur Staff, February 21, 2017.

3. Daskal, Lolly. The Leadership Gap. Penguin Group, 2017.

My father was a motivator. In grade school I would walk to his store on the main street of our town after school, and often he would be standing in front of the store, smoking a chesterfield, sipping his strong coffee, and trying to motivate the high school students who would come to talk with him, to share their doubts, their problems with parents, girlfriends, academics etc. He was a counselor, a business owner, a husband, a dad, and his personality was always the same. He motivated many young people who would not have gone to college if he had not believed in them. College kids loved working for him; they would drive the furniture truck and I would be the sidekick. Local policemen were often seen sipping coffee in his store on cold days, asking him questions about his thirteen parachute jumps into enemy territory during his time in the OSS, which was the forerunner of the CIA. My dad's business felt like a community business to me. He gave his own form of financing. "You'll pay something today, and the rest when you can." And he had a soft spot for immigrants, for those coming from other countries as his parents had.

My father's business did not make millions. He did make enough to support a family and send me to college. He loved selling and he loved connecting with others, and people still talk about him today. Will your legacy be similar to his? It can be. Success, ethics, integrity and community can be integrated.

## Eulogy Virtues

Years ago, empathy, compassion and high-level interpersonal skills were viewed as soft skills, and not necessary for personal and business success. We know that wealth alone does not make people happy; I treat wealthy people every week who are unhappy and unhealthy.

They have yet to learn that happiness is a by-product of giving; it cannot be pursued directly. Performance addicts have a great deal of trouble accepting this fact. They believe they can perfect their way into happiness and that revenue and possessions will bring them what they continually desire.

In my consultations with corporations I have consistently encountered depleted leaders who are excelling financially but have little idea about what is interfering with experiencing personal happiness. Their ability to sustain intimacy in their marriages, with their children and with friends is significantly compromised.

I often ask leaders to contemplate what people will say at their funeral, and how those comments relate to what is stated in their resumes. Many accomplished, successful individuals can describe what they have done in their lives, but when it comes to describing who they are, and what they have meant to other people, their responses are typically tentative and vague.

If you Google empathy and businesses you will get 30 million results. We know, as a result of many studies, that empathy and character are intimately linked to business results. Knowing is theoretical, implementing requires a leader whose character and communication skills create an exciting environment that not only creates desired results, but generates deep, unforgettable connections and experiences that permeate throughout their organization.

I hope the ideas in this book will provide you with a guide to leading *soulfully*. I also hope that your efforts will touch the hearts and minds of your employees in a manner that makes them get up every morning wanting to come to work and be a soulful contributor to a greater cause.

# Recommended Reading

Bennett, T. *The Power of Storytelling: The Art of Influential Communication*. Utah. Sound Concepts, Inc.

Brennan, J. *The Art of Becoming Oneself*. Tarentum, PA. Word Association, 2011

Breuning-Graziano, Loretta. *Habits of a Happy Brain: Retrain Your Brain to Boost Your Serotonin, Dopamine, Oxytocin and Endorphin Levels*. Avon, Massachusetts. Adams Media, 2016

Burg, B. and Mann, J.D. *The Go-Giver Leader*. UK. Penguin/Random House, 2016

Ciaramicoli, Arthur. *The Stress Solution: Using Empathy and Cognitive Behavioral Therapy to Reduce Anxiety and Develop Resilience*. Novato, California. New World Library, 2016

Ciaramicoli, Arthur. *Performance Addiction: The Dangerous New Syndrome and How to Stop it From Ruining Your Life*. Hoboken, NJ. Wiley, 2004

Ciaramicoli, Arthur, and Katherine Ketcham. *The Power of Empathy: A Practical Guide to Creating Intimacy, Self-understanding, and Lasting Love*. New York, Plume. 2000

Dalia Lama and Tutu, Desmond. *The Book of Joy*.

New York. Avery, 2016

Emmons, Robert. *Thanks: How Practicing Gratitude Can Make You Happier*. Boston: Houghton Mifflin Company, 2008

Gallo, Carmine. *Talk Like Ted: The 9 Public-Speaking Secretes of the World's Top Minds*. New York. St. Martin's Press

Goleman, Daniel. *Emotional Intelligence: Why It Can Matter More Than IQ*. New York. Bantam, 199

Goleman, Daniel. *Working with Emotional Intelligence*. New York: Bantam, 1998

Ketcham, Kathy and Kurtz, Ernest. *The Spirituality of Imperfection: Storytelling and the Journey to Wholeness*. New York: Bantam, 1994

Klein, Stephen. *The Science of Happiness*. New York: Marlowe, 2002

Kolts, Rand and Chodran, T. *An Open Hearted Life*. Boston: Shambala, 2015

Korb, Alex. *The Upward Spiral: Using Neuroscience to Reverse the Course of Depression, One Small Change at a Time*. Oakland: New Harbinger Publications, 2015

Marquez, Xavier. "This is why authoritarian leaders use the 'Big Lie'". *The Washington Post*, 1/26/2017

Myers, David. *The American Paradox: Hunger in an Age of Plenty*. New Haven, Connecticut. Yale University Press, 2000

Pepinsky, Thomas. *Economic Crisis and the Breakdown of Authoritative Regimes*. London: Cambridge University Press, 2009

Pelletier, Kenneth. *Sound Mind, Sound Body*. New York. Fireside, 1995

Petterson, Jordan. *12 Rules For Life: An Antidote to Chaos*. London. Allen Lane, 2018

Pfeffer, Jeffrey. *Why Deception Is Probably the Single Most Important Leadership Skill. Fortune Magazine*, 6/2/2016

Rohr, Richard. *Falling Upward: Spirituality for the Two Halves of Life*. New York: Josey-Bass, 2011

Rohr, Richard. *Simplicity: The Freedom of Letting Go*. New York: Crossroad, 2003

Scalavitz, Maia and Perry, Bruce. *Born for Love: Why Empathy is Essential and Endangered*. New York: William Morrow, 2010

Spaulding, Tommy. *The Heart Led Leader: How Living and Leading from the Heart Will Change Your Organization and Your Life*. New York: Crow Business, 2015

Thayer, Robert. *Calm Energy: How People Regulate Mood with Food and Exercise*. New York: Oxford University Press, 2001

# About the Authors

ARTHUR P. CIARAMICOLI, ED.D., PH.D., is a licensed clinical psychologist who has been treating clients for more than 35 years. He is a member of the American Psychological Association and the Massachusetts Psychological Association.

Dr. Ciaramicoli is a contributor to The Creative Living Foundation, is on the faculty of The International Association of Wellness Practitioners, was formerly the Chief Medical Officer of Soundmindz. org and is also in private practice. Dr. Ciaramicoli has been on the faculty of Harvard Medical School for several years, lecturer for the American Cancer Society, Chief Psychologist at Metrowest Medical Center, and Director of the Metrowest Counseling Center and of the Alternative Medicine division of Metrowest Wellness Center in Framingham, Massachusetts.

In addition to treating patients, Dr. Ciaramicoli has lectured at Harvard Health Services, Boston College Counseling Center, the Space Telescope Science Institute in Baltimore, The Revelry Group as well as being a consultant to several major corporations in the Boston area.

Dr. Ciaramicoli has appeared on CNN, CNNfn, Fox News Boston, Comcast TV, New England Cable News, Good Morning America Weekend, The O'Reilly Report, and other shows. He has been a weekly radio guest on Your Healthy Family on Sirius Satellite Radio and Holistic Health Today, and has been interviewed on more than two dozen other radio programs airing on NPR, XM Radio, and numerous AM and FM stations.

Dr. Ciaramicoli is the author of *The Stress Solution: Using Empathy and Cognitive Behavioral Therapy to Reduce Anxiety and Develop Resilience* (New World Library, 2014) which has just been published in China. He also authored *Performance Addiction: The Dangerous New Syndrome* and *How to Stop It from Ruining Your Life* (Wiley 2004), *The Curse of the Capable: The Hidden Challenges to a Balanced, Healthy, High Achieving Life* (Wiley, 2010),and *The Power of Empathy: A Practical Guide to Creating Intimacy, Self-Understanding, and Lasting Love* (Dutton 2000), which is now published in 7 languages, most recently making the best seller list at #8 in newly published psychological books in China.

Dr. Ciaramicoli's first book, *Treatment of Abuse and Addiction, A Holistic Approach* (Jason Aronson, 1997) was selected as Book of the Month by The Psychotherapy Book News. He is also the co-author of *Beyond the Influence: Understanding and Defeating Alcoholism* (Bantam 2000) and founder of The Empathy and Goodness Project on Facebook and Healthy Empathic Achievement on LinkedIn.

He has also authored the Anti-Anxiety app, Anti-Depression App and workbooks *Transforming Anxiety into Joy: A Practical Workbook to Gain Emotional Freedom* (2012) and *Changing Your Inner Voice: A Journey through Depression to Truth and Love* (2012) in collaboration with Soundmindz.org.

Dr. Ciaramicoli lives in a suburb of Boston with his wife of 37 years. His website is http://www.balanceyoursuccess.com/. His twitter handle is docapc.

Dr. Ciaramicoli enjoys cycling, spinning, and other sports and his favorite activity is spending time with his wife, daughters, sons-in-law and beautiful grandchildren Ariana and Carmela along the southern coast of Maine.

JIM CRYSTAL IS THE founder of The Revelry Group, a company that provides products and services to the food, beverage, and hospitality industry. Jim started his career working for fortune 500 companies and received best in class leadership training as a manager and leader. After starting Revelry, Jim began consulting for fortune 500 companies at the C-level and found there was consistency across all the organizations—their stated culture and actual culture were at odds due to the demands placed on management to attain targets. These companies aspired to be something better, but the pressures of meeting numbers always swept aside values and behaviors in order to meet financial expectations. After studying the B corporation movement, Jim structured The Revelry Group to ensure that the values of the company could not be compromised under any circumstances, and that the business would always be a force for good.

**The Revelry Group** is a company focused on Food, Beverage, and Hospitality. The company has three divisions: Marketing Services, Conferences, and Beverage Manufacturing.

Revelry's marketing services were the first division in the company. Revelry does traditional marketing communications for food/beverage manufacturers and hospitality chains. Clients in this space are Marriott, Choice Hotels, Nestle, Hershey, Schwan's, Idahoan, State of Alaska, and a number of others.

Revelry's conferences, or Exchanges, happen 6 times per year: one for CEO's, one for CMO's, one for CFO's, and three for purchasing and R&D. All are targeted at the large chain operator with manufacturers as the sponsors. This year the company will host over 100 hotel/restaurant chains and 100 food/beverage manufacturers across all 6 conferences. These companies represent the biggest in the industry at a C-level.

# Appendix

## AIG Leadership Questionnaires

Please answer yes or no to the following questions and compare your answers to the first time you took this questionnaire. Please be as honest as possible.

### Authenticity

1. My behavior is always consistent with my values.

   Yes  No

2. I value establishing genuine relationships through-out my life.

   Yes  No

3. I seldom try to project a false image of myself.

   Yes  No

4. My employees and family know they can depend on me because my values always guide my actions.

   Yes  No

5. I consult others when making major decisions and my ultimate opinion reflects my values.

   Yes  No

6. My employees are high spirited because they know I am genuinely interested in their work and their lives.

Yes  No

7. I am open to truthful feedback from my employees.

Yes  No

8. The standards I set for myself are the same as those for my team.

Yes  No

9. I have spent many years trying to understand myself and I will continue to do so throughout my life.

Yes  No

10. I am comfortable expressing my feelings.

Yes  No

11. I seek honest feedback from all I employ, not just my peers.

Yes  No

12. I am clear as to how I go about making decisions.

Yes  No

13. I am keenly aware of the role model I set for my company/institution.

Yes  No

14. I am committed to allow time to understand and respond to my staff's concerns.

Yes  No

15. I am not uncomfortable revealing my weaknesses.

    Yes  No

16. I am committed to listening to the points of view of employees I don't agree with.

    Yes  No

17. I do not allow 'group think' to dominate what I think.

    Yes  No

18. I am not uncomfortable to express my strengths.

    Yes  No

19. My values are integrated in my personal and professional life.

    Yes  No

20. I believe the people in my life make my life whole.

    Yes  No

21. I am keenly aware how my personality affects those I encounter.

    Yes  No

22. I am fully present with I talk to others in my life.

    Yes  No

23. I am the same person at work and at home.

    Yes  No

24. I seek consultation before I make major decisions.

    Yes  No

25. I believe humility is central to strong leadership.

Yes  No

26. I am not arrogance and boastful.

Yes  No

27. I do not value aggression as a means of influencing others.

Yes  No

28. I do not interrupt co-workers but rather listen carefully to the perspectives of employees.

Yes  No

29. I am generally content with who I am.

Yes  No

30. I know how to turn the dial down and calm myself.

Yes  No

31. I work hard to achieve and make a meaningful difference rather than to boost self-esteem.

Yes  No

32. I am passionate about my work; I enjoy the process and the people.

Yes  No

33. I seldom wish I had chosen a different vocation.

Yes  No

34. I seldom rehearse what I am going to say while listening to others.

Yes  No

35. I would not rather be at work than being with my family.

    Yes  No

36. I know how to make and maintain meaningful relationships.

    Yes  No

37. I will make time for family events, school meetings, and children's games despite needing to miss work time

    Yes  No

38. I do not become impulsive or aggressive when in the face of conflict.

    Yes  No

39. I am living according to my beliefs and values, seldom being influenced by the need to impress.

    Yes  No

40. I seldom let work pressure influence my personal relationships.

    Yes  No

41. I am seldom so busy that I stop taking care of myself and those close to me.

    Yes  No

42. I seldom fantasize about being a more powerful person.

    Yes  No

43. I am seldom anxious about how people perceive me.

Yes No

44. I seldom act in ways to gain the approval of others.

Yes No

45. I generally have high energy and enthusiasm; I look forward to each day.

Yes No

46. I seldom behave in a manner that is not healthy for me or those close to me.

Yes No

47. I feel in control of my life and seldom feel that I am being directed by outside forces.

Yes No

## Assessment

4 or less "No" Answers: Very Authentic

9-10 "No" Answers: Somewhat Authentic

20-25 "No" Answers: Inauthentic

Above 25 "No" Answers: Complete Lack of Authenticity

## Integrity

1. Are you forthcoming regarding the financial status of your company?

Yes No

2. Do you remain truthful when you know if you distorted the truth it would increase profits?

Yes No

3. When hiring employees do you give a factual presentation of your company's future?

Yes  No

4. Do you adhere to company policies regardless of your status in your company?

Yes  No

5. Do you consider yourself more ethical than your colleagues in the business world?

Yes  No

6. Would you refrain from altering the truth even if stretching the truth may gain your company a desirable contract?

Yes  No

7. Even though this survey is anonymous are you committed to telling the truth?

Yes  No

8. Have you ever omitted or distorted facts on your tax return?

Yes  No

9. Have you ever lied about your child's age to save money?

Yes  No

10. Do you give honest feedback when dismissing an employee?

Yes  No

11. Do you tell the truth when your children asks you about your past?

Yes  No

12. Do you tell the truth when asked about your work history?

Yes  No

13. Do you maintain proper boundaries with employees of the opposite sex?

Yes  No

14. Did you answer the previous question honestly?

Yes  No

15. If you are uncomfortable answering these questions would you acknowledge your anxiety to someone close to you?

Yes  No

16. Do you give honest reasons for your absence from work?

Yes  No

17. Do you tell your spouse, significant other the truth when asked about your stress at work?

Yes  No

18. If you were overpaid on your weekly check would you inform human resources?

Yes  No

19. Do you think it is dishonest to fudge your expense reports?

Yes  No

20. Do you think the by laws of your company apply

to you as well those below you?

Yes  No

21. Did you answer the last question honestly?

Yes  No

22. Would you decline to write a reference for a close friend if you knew the candidate was unqualified?

Yes  No

23. Would you decline to hire a friend if you knew he/she was unqualified?

Yes  No

24. Would you decline to use someone else's content for a presentation even though it is quite unlikely that the content source would be identified?

Yes  No

25. If a vendor forgot to bill your company would you take action to remind the vendor to bill your company accurately?

Yes  No

26. If you accidentally nicked another person's car in a parking lot would you leave a note saying so?

Yes  No

27. Did you answer the previous question honestly?

Yes  No

28. Would you object to colleagues shading the truth even if it may mean losing a profitable contract?

Yes  No

29. Do you believe sound ethics and character are necessary for business success?

Yes  No

30. Would you continue to employ a high revenue earner even though he or she behaves in unethical manners?

Yes  No

31. Do you believe your business/institution is one that exudes honesty throughout all levels of employees?

Yes  No

32. Do you seldom wake during the night thinking of an act of dishonesty on your part?

Yes  No

33. Do you believe your decisions are value based?

Yes  No

34. Do you refrain from exaggeration when meeting with a potential customer?

Yes  No

35. When business is hurting would you cover up the negative facts to those you lead?

Yes  No

36. Do you keep your commitment to customers even after contracts are signed?

Yes  No

37. Do you refrain from using your staff for personal reasons?

Yes  No

38. If you found a $100 bill on the basement floor of a parking garage would you tell the attendant of the hotel?

    Yes  No

39. Would you attend to a small customer's legitimate complaint as you would to a large customer's complaint?

    Yes  No

40. Do you let people know when you can't accommodate their needs rather than making false promises?

    Yes  No

41. Did you answer the previous question honestly?

    Yes  No

42. Do you tell the truth when you cancel meetings with employees or family when you know it will lead to disappointment?

    Yes  No

43. Would you be truthful when pulled over by a state trooper for speeding rather than making up a story?

    Yes  No

44. Would you refuse to support an unethical political candidate even though he or she could help your company gain lucrative contracts?

    Yes  No

## Assessment

4 or less "No" Answers: Stellar Integrity

9-10 "No" Answers: Fair Integrity

20-25 "No" Answers: Low Integrity

Above 25 "No" Answers: Complete Lack of Integrity

## Empathy

1. I have been told that I lack empathy by more than one person.

   Yes  No

2. I have been told that I am empathic by more than one person.

   Yes  No

3. I feel good when I help another person.

   Yes  No

4. I don't feel much when I help another person.

   Yes  No

5. I feel obligated to do the right thing.

   Yes  No

6. I enjoy giving of my time to others.

   Yes  No

7. I am uncomfortable when people talk about emotional issues.

   Yes  No

8. I am not uncomfortable when people talk about emotional issues.

   Yes  No

9. I don't know what it means to express empathy.

    Yes  No

10. I understand what it means to express empathy.

    Yes  No

11. I often feel that I miss emotional cues.

    Yes  No

12. I pick up emotional cues easily.

    Yes  No

13. I have been told that I need to be right.

    Yes  No

14. I don't place much value on the need to be right.

    Yes  No

15. I seldom talk beyond the surface with friends.

    Yes  No

16. My friends and I have deep conversations.

    Yes  No

17. I prefer to not be around young children.

    Yes  No

18. I love being around young children.

    Yes  No

19. I think I tend to take more than I give.

    Yes  No

20. I think I tend to give more than I take.

Yes  No

21. I find it easier to show animals affection rather than people.

Yes  No

22. I can give affection to animals and people equally.

Yes  No

23. I have often been called stubborn.

Yes  No

24. I am often told that I am easy to get along with.

Yes  No

25. I prefer to talk more than listen.

Yes  No

26. I prefer to listen more than talk.

Yes  No

27. In most of my conversations I talk more than I listen.

Yes  No

28. In most of my conversations I listen more than I talk.

Yes  No

29. I am uncomfortable getting close to people.

Yes  No

30. I feel comfortable being close to people.

Yes  No

## Assessment

Give yourself one point for saying "Yes" to any of the following questions:

#2,3,6,8,10,12,14,16,18,20,22,24,26,28 and 30.

Take away one point for saying "Yes" to any of the following questions:

#1,5,7,9,11,13,15,17,19,21,23,25, and 29.

**Total Number:**
**Very Empathic: 13-15**
**Mildly Empathic: 10-12**
**Low Empathy: 0-7**

## The Performance Addiction Questionnaire

Instructions: Use this self-scoring quiz to measure the level of possible performance addiction you may have. To score, add one point for every "Yes" answer.

1. Did you seldom feel listened to as a child?

   Yes  No

2. Did you worry that if you didn't please your parents you would lose their love?

   Yes  No

3. Did you question whether your parents truly loved each other?

   Yes  No

4. Did you often feel guilty?

   Yes  No

5. Did you seldom have fun with your parents out-side of achievement-oriented situations?

Yes  No

6. Were your parents quite conscious of your physical appearance?

Yes  No

7. Did you experience one or both parents as critical people in general?

Yes  No

8. Do you have memories of specific childhood hurts that have never left you?

Yes  No

9. Were you easily humiliated as a young person?

Yes  No

10. Were you considered to be a very sensitive child?

Yes  No

11. Do you believe your past mistakes make you unlovable today?

Yes  No

12. Do you want unconditional acceptance, with no criticism?

Yes  No

13. Do you feel irritated when people close to you are not being capable and efficient?

Yes  No

14. Do you always have a to-do list in your mind or in your pocket?

    Yes  No

15. Have you considered or have you already had cosmetic surgery?

    Yes  No

16. Are you chronically dissatisfied with the way people respond to you?

    Yes  No

17. Do you often feel you have to work much harder than others to excel?

    Yes  No

18. Do you wonder if anyone really loves anyone else for who they are rather than for what they do?

    Yes  No

19. Are you frequently trying to perfect the way you speak?

    Yes  No

20. Are you frequently trying to perfect your appearance?

    Yes  No

21. Do you often discover that people are far less critical than you imagined?

    Yes  No

22. Do you have trouble tolerating your own imperfections?

    Yes  No

23. Do you have trouble tolerating others' imperfections?

Yes  No

24. Do you often wonder how much money others make?

Yes  No

25. When friends, relatives, or colleagues have success, do you feel you don't measure up?

Yes  No

26. Are you unable to stop perfectionist thinking even though you know it's irrational?

Yes  No

27. Are you afraid that if you were not so driven you would be lazy?

Yes  No

28. Do you feel guilty if you just hang out and do nothing?

Yes  No

29. Are you afraid of trying to learn new things for fear of being humiliated?

Yes  No

30. Deep down, do you think you're "not much"?

Yes  No

31. No matter what you think of yourself, do you find that you can't stop thinking about yourself?

Yes  No

32. Does your self-voice tend to be punitive rather than understanding?

Yes  No

33. Do you tend to generalize about yourself in a negative way under stress? (Do you say things to yourself like "I'm so stupid!" or "I'm so fat!"?)

Yes  No

34. Are you seldom content to be with one person in one place for very long?

Yes  No

35. Are you easily bored in conversation?

Yes  No

36. Does your energy pick up when the conversation is about you?

Yes  No

37. Do you like being idealized by others?

Yes  No

38. Do you tend to idealize others?

Yes  No

39. Do you feel pressured to impress others in order to secure their love?

Yes  No

40. Do you fear that loss of status will lead to loss of love?

Yes  No

41. Are you afraid you don't know what true love really is?

Yes  No

42. Have you seldom felt loved the way you want to be loved?

    Yes  No

43. Is it difficult for you to truly trust others?

    Yes  No

44. Do you question whether you have true friends?

    Yes  No

45. Are you afraid your long-term love relationship is based on what you do for each other rather than a deeper sense of love?

    Yes  No

46. Do you have sexual relations infrequently?

    Yes  No

47. Are you seldom "present in the moment" during sex?

    Yes  No

48. Do you weigh yourself daily?

    Yes  No

49. Are you intolerant of weight gain?

    Yes  No

50. Are you intolerant of the aging process?

    Yes  No

51. Do you imagine if you could perfect certain body parts your life would be dramatically improved?

    Yes  No

52. Do you compare your financial situation to others?

    Yes  No

53. Do you notice the cars people drive and rate those people accordingly?

    Yes  No

54. Do you feel uncomfortable and less worthy in a home that is larger and more extravagant than your own?

    Yes  No

55. Do have a sense of inferiority in relation to people who have more education than you?

    Yes  No

56. Do you tend to attach certain personality characteristics to those who attended prestigious schools?

    Yes  No

57. Do you rank people according to the affluence of the town or city where they live?

    Yes  No

58. Do you feel deprived when a neighbor or friend has a more attractive spouse than yours?

    Yes  No

59. Do you fantasize about being with someone who is far more attractive than your spouse or lover?

    Yes  No

60. Do you think that if you were more attractive you would be with a different spouse or lover?

    Yes  No

61. Do you think that if you were more successful financially you would be with a different spouse or lover?

Yes  No

62. Do you tend to think that others have had an unfair advantage in terms of the success they have achieved?

Yes  No

63. Do you measure another person's success apart from the quality of that person's relationships?

Yes  No

64. Do you measure success without giving much weight to a person's character?

Yes  No

65. Assuming that you know how to care for your body, do you find that you are seldom consistent with your self-care measures?

Yes  No

66. Do you exercise too little or too much?

Yes  No

67. Are you on a diet at least once every year?

Yes  No

68. At least once a week, do you have three or more alcoholic drinks in a single day?

Yes  No

69. Do you take sleep aids monthly or more often?

Yes  No

70. Do you consider exercise and proper sleep and nutritional habits low priorities in your life?

    Yes  No

71. Do you drink more than three caffeinated beverages per day?

    Yes  No

72. Do you often eat comfort foods, especially in the evening?

    Yes  No

73. Do you seldom think about the quality of your relationships?

    Yes  No

74. With each passing year, do you think you become less desirable to others?

    Yes  No

Add up the total number of points and use the following to rate the level of your performance addiction: Score your level of "Yes" answers to determine your level of performance addiction.

**60+ Severe; 50-59 Significant; 40-49 Moderate; 30-39 Mild; 20-29 Low.**

# Acknowledgements

I HAVE BEEN VERY fortunate to always have the enduring love and support of my family, friends and colleagues. My wife Karen has always believed in me and the value of my work. Her support and love as the leader of our family is un-paralleled. Our daughters Erica and Alaina have been more loving to me than any father could possibly expect. I thank you both for the pride I take in the greatest experience I have ever had—being your Dad.

Their husbands Michael MacDonald and Michael Chagnon are equally supportive and loving. Our granddaughters Ariana and Carmela are the angels that bring me incredible joy every week, providing me with the motivation to try to make our world and their world better.

My constant supporters Gerri and Richard Tessicini, Donna and Philip Wood, Janice and Jimmy Blackler, Drs. Valerie and Peter Smith and Dr. Robert Cherney and his wife Mary Ellen have encouraged me throughout the writing of this book.

Thank you to Larry Brady of Cortland State College for the many invaluable conversations regarding ethical leadership. Your students are very fortunate to have a faculty member who cares so deeply about their future.

A very special thank you to coach Brain Kelly, a soulful leader of young men, for taking the time in the midst of the college championship series to write a poignant foreword to this book.

Thank you to Luke Kircher, President of the Revelry group for introducing me to the AIE leadership of the Revelry group. And to Jim Crystal, Founder of the Revelry group, for his encouragement and insightful review of the original text.

A special thank you to David Ross, my editor at Open Books, who gave me the opportunity to publish these ideas and provided expert editorial insights that have made this book flow in a manner I could not have accomplished on my own. I also thank Kelly Huddleston for her editorial help, and especially for her insightful ideas on how to have this book reach the largest possible audience.

Lastly, I thank the numerous leaders who have joined my leadership and communication groups, and who are committed to making their organizations AIE environments. Your courage to be open and vulnerable led to the insights revealed in this book.

Made in the USA
Lexington, KY
02 March 2019